KU-192-504

Book 3: Law and Politics
and Law in the Colonies

LAW, CLASS AND SOCIETY

Book 3:
Law and Politics
and
Law in the Colonies

by

D. N. PRITT

"In Politics there is no honour"
BENJAMIN DISRAELI

1971
LAWRENCE AND WISHART
LONDON

Copyright © D. N. Pritt, 1971

SBN: 85315 242

Printed in Great Britain
by the Camelot Press Ltd.,
London and Southampton

Introduction

This is the third of my four Books written under the collective heading of "Law, Class and Society", in which I consider the role of the law and the lawyers in the class struggle—both the way in which the law has been shaped and re-shaped by the conflicting pressures of the ruling class of the time and of the workers, and the roles which judges, lawyers, and the legislature have played in the actual struggle.

In the first Book, "Employers, Workers and Trade Unions", published in 1970, I dealt with the centuries of struggle in the wage-labour relation, and the formation and advance of the trade union movement, all of which give many illustrations of the conflicts—unending under the capitalist system—between those who work for wages and those who employ them, and of the parts played therein by judges, lawyers and the legislature.

In my second Book, "The Apparatus of the Law", published in 1971, I considered, always from the point of view of the class struggle, the sources of our law and the manner in which it has been and still is being built up, the judges, the magistrates, juries, and lawyers, and the actual operation of the law in the Courts.

In the present Book, I deal with two matters. The first is that of the directly political aspects and activities of the Law, i.e., the law and legislation which are in reality "political", dealing with the powers and activities of governments in fields where they face political opposition from the population, and in particular with the highly significant fashion in which political prosecutions are conducted and defended. The second is that of the application of the law in colonial territories, which has thrown—and to some extent still throws—a vivid light on the manner in which our ruling class behaves in its government of peoples ill equipped to resist its greed for profit.

In the fourth and final Book of the series, I hope to deal, in the same way and from the same point of view, with the law of property, the law of personal relations, the law of contract and tort, the police and the armed forces, and the topic of civil liberties.

Contents

Contents

Part One

LAW AND POLITICS

I

Political Law

By political law I mean those provisions of the Common Law*
and of Acts of Parliament which are pretty directly aimed at the
repression of activities regarded by the ruling class as pre-
judicial to the maintenance of its power, and to what it calls
"the state"—what many people call the establishment. Fright-
ened members of the ruling class often call it "the Constitution",
a vague phrase which I discussed in Chapter 6 of Book 2; this
enables them to denounce their opponents and terrify the un-
thinking without the trouble and difficulty of formulating any
precise statement of what they mean. When, for example, Sir
John Simon—as he then was—attacked the General Strike of
1926 as "unconstitutional", I doubt whether anyone (except
perhaps Simon himself, who if one believed him could explain
anything) could have explained what he meant.

By political cases, I mean prosecutions for alleged breaches
of some provision of one or more of these political laws or for
alleged breaches of some provision of the general—the ordinary
—law, such as, say, the law that makes assaults criminal, when
committed for clearly political motives. (The governments of
many countries, including our own, assert that there is no such
thing as a political case, or political law, although they would
probably admit that treason would fall within the definition.
And most countries, including Britain, try their political cases,
major or minor,† in their ordinary Courts. But West Germany,

---

* The Common Law, as I explained in Chapter 2 of Book 2, is that large part
of our law, civil and criminal, which has been gradually built up over the centuries
by the judgments of our Courts, and not just created by Acts of Parliament.

† I explained in Chapter 8 of Book 2 the distinction between major and minor
cases. The former are the more serious cases, which come before the magistrates
only to determine whether the prosecution has made out a case sufficient to be sent
for trial to Quarter Sessions or Assizes, where they must be tried with a jury; and
the latter are that immense majority of cases which can be tried "at one go" before
magistrates, sitting without a jury and having power to convict "off their own bat".

the "Federal Republic of Germany", which brings tens of thousands of political prosecutions every year, is less hypocritical than some; it appoints special "political divisions" of many of its Courts exclusively for the trial of political cases.)

It does not matter very much whether our or any other government can justify the assertion that it has no political law or political cases; the essence of the matter is that in many countries honest citizens, in no sense rightly or normally to be classified as criminals acting anti-socially and deserving imprisonment, are frequently tried for and convicted of alleged crimes because they have exercised their rights as citizens to protest, or argue, or demonstrate on political issues.

I shall proceed to state the content of our political law. As those who have read the two previous books will realise, this law forms a disorderly jumble of relics from different periods of our history, difficult even to classify. I will do what I can to state them comprehensibly. I can omit for present purposes the trade union legislation with which I dealt fully in Book 1, and can take the rest of the political laws one by one. The first and gravest of them, although no longer the most important in practice, is the law of Treason. In spite of a good many efforts to simplify it, the law of treason is still a pretty bewildering jumble of common law and statute. As it stands today, its main heads are:

1. Compassing the death of the King, the Queen, or their eldest son and heir;

2. "Levying war against the King in his realm", which has been extended to cover matters far removed from war. Many activities which in ordinary language would be called riots have been held to be treason—even when carried on by small numbers and without military weapons—if they were directed against some general or national grievance as distinct from local ones;

3. "Adhering to the King's enemies, giving them aid and comfort in the realm or elsewhere"; it was under this head that Sir Roger Casement was convicted in the First World War.

I need not write of treason at any greater length, for prosecutions for this crime are rare, and most of those who are likely to be guilty of it are members of the ruling class, whom the government will be reluctant to prosecute; I shall give a remarkable illustration of this in Chapter 4.

The next political offence to be examined is that of Sedition, an offence created by the Common Law; like many common law offences, it is difficult to state shortly or accurately, and is dangerously elastic in its interpretation and application. The best statement which one can distil from the many authorities is that sedition consists of words written and published, or spoken, with a "seditious intention", and that this seditious intention, which can be inferred from the words themselves or proved from other evidence, pretty clearly comprises five heads, of varying importance.

The first is the intention to bring into hatred or contempt, or to excite disaffection against, the Queen (our monarch being at present a female), the Government and Constitution —again, this vague word—of the United Kingdom, or either House of Parliament, or the administration of justice; but the case law makes some limitation of this positive statement by laying down that it is not seditious merely to attempt to show that the Queen has been misled or mistaken in her measures, or to point out errors or defects in the government or constitution with a view to their reformation. This combination of positive assertion, and half-contradictory qualification, built up by a series of decisions, shows how the Courts, at different times and dealing with different allegedly seditious words, have sought on the one hand to serve governments who wanted to repress opposition, and on the other hand to respect, or at least to pay lip-service to, the oft-proclaimed right of the public to freedom of speech, writing, and criticism (and, occasionally, actually to help the opponents of a government which the judges disliked).

The second head of seditious intention is the intention to excite the Queen's subjects to attempt, otherwise than by lawful means, "the alteration of any matter in Church or State by law established"—another conveniently vague provision of very little present-day applicability.

The third is the intention to incite persons to commit any crime "in general disturbance of the peace".

The fourth—and here we reach a more important and more

frequently arising point of danger for critics of the establishment—is the intention to arouse discontent or dissatisfaction amongst the Queen's subjects; and the fifth, still more important and more dangerous, is the intention to promote feelings of ill-will and hostility between different classes of the Queen's subjects. On this head there are again limitations laying down that it is lawful to point out, with a view to their removal, matters which are producing or have a tendency to produce feelings of hatred or ill-will between different classes of the Queen's subjects. There ·is, moreover, some authority for the proposition that no offence is committed under this head unless the words are of such a nature as to promote disorder as a result of such feelings of ill-will.*

The law of sedition, as I have just stated it—and I think most lawyers of any or no political views would probably agree with my exposition—is, as can be seen, extremely vague. If it were strictly interpreted and applied, it would render criminal nearly all progressive political propaganda; it was indeed described, in the case of Tom Mann to which I have just referred, by a police officer whom I cross-examined, as "saying anything of which I disapprove". One can imagine that many politicians would, if it were explained to them, say—as Monsieur Jourdain said of prose—that they had been talking sedition all their lives without knowing it. Even the late Professor Dicey, an ultra-conservative lawyer of three-quarters of a century ago, wrote of it: "The legal definition of sedition might easily be used to assist to check a great deal of what is ordinarily considered allowable discussion, and would if rigidly enforced be inconsistent with the prevailing forms of political agitation."

The vagueness of the law of sedition is typical of much of the common law, and indeed of Acts of Parliament too, including much of the trade union law which I discussed in Book 1, in the field of "keeping the masses in their place". This vagueness is a valuable weapon of the cunning ruling class. It

---

* The judge who tried the charge of sedition against Tom Mann, which I describe below, in Chapter 4, a judge of rare impartiality, said to me, when he came into Court to try the case and saw a row of Law Reports lying on the desk in front of me: "Mr. Pritt, what do you need all those books for?" I told him of this point, and he replied: "You will not need the books, for I shall direct the jury that that is the law."

enables it, on the one hand, to "ride on a light rein" when dealing with members of its own class, or even with their opponents in a quiet period (and so to avoid raising demands for repeal or amendment of some political laws), and, on the other hand, when any emergency arises, to prosecute for words or actions that should never be treated as criminal. The ruling class can always rely on the judges, in the atmosphere of any emergency, to rule that some speech or pamphlet can be found by a jury to be seditious, and on the jury to find that it is. And all the while, in quiet times and in stormy, the law of sedition, like that of libel, to which I will devote a Chapter in Book 4, operates silently to prohibit the publication of much that would not in fact be prosecuted if someone took the risk of publishing it. Progressive writers who want to say something which they regard as socially valuable but do not want to go to prison if they can fairly remain free will often ask their lawyers if they can write this or that with impunity, only to find that the law is so vague that even the best and most sympathetic of lawyers is forced to give them nothing better than vague and hesitant advice, as a result of which they will often refrain from writing, and their printers will still more often refuse to risk printing, matter which is important for the public to read and is not in truth seditious at all. Thus governments silently and passively secure all the advantages which a successful prosecution would have brought, without incurring the trouble, expense and odium of prosecuting, or the danger of the accused being acquitted.

It may be wondered why, with all these advantages, prosecutions for sedition are comparatively rare nowadays, and were rare even in the colonies, where the normal English boasts about freedom of expression of opinion were never made. Indeed, what one usually heard from colonial officials, when one protested to them against prosecutions for sedition (or, more often, criminal libel) being brought in respect of words which no one would dream of prosecuting in England, was: "You just do not understand, old boy. This isn't Britain, and it isn't safe to let people here publish the sort of thing that is tolerated at home. We simply can't allow it." (And it was no good telling them that that was the way to lose the "Empire". They "knew better"; but they lost it.)

One reason for the rarity of such prosecutions is that they cannot be brought summarily and disposed of by the magistrates, but have to go to the Assizes, which means that the government cannot get a decision quickly, or cheaply, and has to take the risk of a jury acquitting the accused. Another reason is that juries prove to be unexpectedly reluctant to convict of sedition. This applies not only to the case of prosecutions that are obviously oppressive, but equally to those rare cases where the prosecution is actually meritorious. In 1947, when I and others were trying hard, both publicly and privately, to make the Labour government legislate against fascism and anti-semitism, and it was retorting that the existing law was sufficient to deal with the problem, it launched a prosecution for sedition against the owner of a newspaper who had published a crude anti-semitic article, advocating violence against Jews, and insisted that the prosecution would succeed, and would demonstrate that no further legislation was needed. We had to wait some time for the case to come to trial, and the jury acquitted the accused. (The case is more fully narrated in the second volume of my *Autobiography*, "Brasshats and Bureaucrats", at pp. 57–8).

I have myself defended seven or eight cases of sedition, including some in the colonies, and have secured acquittals in all of them—in sharp contrast to the normal experience of political defences, as I shall describe in Chapter 4 below, where one scarcely ever expects to win.

There are still some common law political offences to consider before I come to Acts of Parliament. I will take next the group of offences called "unlawful assembly, rout, and riot", which were long important in times of industrial trouble, and are still of some importance, and likely to increase in importance, since political demonstrations are growing more frequent and are regularly broken up by the police, with prosecutions to follow. It is true, as we shall see below, that the modern tendency is to prosecute the participants in the police Courts for minor offences against various minor statutory regulations which are called "policemen's friends". But the more serious charges are still used, and I will turn to them. An unlawful assembly is an assembly of three or more persons intending either to commit a crime by open force or to carry out any common purpose, even a perfectly lawful one, in such a manner as to give to firm and courageous persons in the neighbourhood reasonable ground to anticipate a breach of the peace. To take part in such an assembly, even before it has moved to the execution of its purpose, is a criminal offence, punishable by fine and imprisonment (theoretically unlimited in point of time, but in practice limited to two years).

The next offence in the group is Rout; it is unimportant, and covers only the moment when an unlawful assembly has started —but no more than started—to move to the execution of its purpose; as soon as the assembly gets any further than that, it is no longer a rout, but becomes a Riot. (Rout is subject to the same punishment as unlawful assembly.)

Riot (which also carries the same penalty) is in effect an unlawful assembly which is actually carrying out its purpose; but it is generally defined as a tumultuous disturbance of the peace by three or more persons who assemble together without lawful authority with an intent mutually to aid one another against any who oppose them in the execution of some purpose (even lawful in itself) and who actually begin to execute their purpose in a violent manner to the terror of the people. The extreme vagueness of these provisions, like those I have already noticed in this and the two previous books, makes it easy for governments in times of tension to secure convictions on very flimsy evidence.

In connection with the law of riot, I should explain the origin of the phrase "Reading the Riot Act", which often puzzles laymen. Its history is illuminating. Early in the reign of George I, in 1714, the government, always apt, like many later governments, to invoke "Law and Order",* was worried over legal difficulties in dispersing unlawful assemblies or riots. It was true of·course that the police, such as they were, and the troops, could be used to disperse any crowd or demonstration

---

* Appeals to "Law and Order" sound most attractive to those who do not think very profoundly about politics. Most people like to move about in peace and quiet, and all of us would prefer to live in an orderly state of society in which the law would be fair and equal in its application to all of us, and would be honestly applied, and where disorder would serve no useful purpose. But such a position cannot arise in a class society, and "law and order" today is the expression of the intention of class governments to repress popular discontent by force rather than remove the cause of discontent. I shall discuss "law and order" more fully in Book 4.

which amounted to an unlawful assembly, and that those taking part could be arrested, tried, convicted and imprisoned; but it was equally true that it was often difficult to find a lawful pretext for firing on them. The difficulty arose from the distinction drawn by the law, as it stood then and until quite recently, between felonies and misdemeanours. Those offences which our ancestors regarded as very serious were felonies under the common law, and any offence which a statute expressly described as a felony of course became one; but offences which were not felonies were only misdemeanours. Subject to certain qualifications, it was lawful to kill people to stop them committing a felony, if that was the only practicable way to stop them, but it was not lawful to kill them merely to stop them committing a misdemeanour. The authorities of that time felt themselves greatly handicapped by the circumstance that unlawful assemblies, routs and riots were only misdemeanours, and that they could therefore not fire on rioters without risk of untoward consequences for themselves, unless the crowd was clearly proceeding to do specific acts which amounted to felony. This was indeed inconvenient from the authorities' point of view; they did not possess modern sophisticated (and "humane") aids like CS gas, and could do little but push unless they had a ground or pretext for shooting. To disperse a crowd by shooting was quick, and apt greatly to diminish the immediate trouble; indeed, it might end it for good, and so avoid the necessity for enquiring into grievances and perhaps even raising wages. Accordingly, the Georgian authorities hit on the bright idea of turning misdemeanours into felonies; they passed the "Riot Act, 1714"—the only statutory interference with the common law position of unlawful assemblies—which provided that if any persons, to the number of twelve or more, are unlawfully, riotously and tumultuously assembled together to the disturbance of the public peace, it is the duty of the justices, or the sheriff, or the mayor (i.e., the persons then entrusted with the maintenance of order) to go to the place where the rioters are assembled and read a proclamation which is set out in the Act—hence the inaccurate but expressive phrase "Reading the Riot Act"—warning them to disperse, and explaining the results of their failing to do so. If thereafter twelve or more persons remain or continue together "unlawfully, riotously and tumultuously" for one hour, the Act makes them felons, and the authorities can shoot them with a clear conscience. If they are killed, they can no longer assemble; if they are not, they are live felons and can be sent to prison for life.

I must next deal with another common law offence, very important and lending itself well to the work of using the criminal law as a weapon against the working class, namely conspiracy. The essence of this—once again, very vaguely stated —offence, with which I dealt pretty fully in Chapter 2 of Book I, is that it constitutes a separate crime the moment that any two or more people have agreed, even tacitly, to commit some crime or even—much more important—any act which, whilst not criminal, is regarded by the Court as particularly objectionable; the crime is complete at the moment the agreement, however made, is made, although no step has been taken towards the criminal or other activity agreed on. The proof of conspiracy is made easier by the provision of the law of evidence (again, common law) that so long as there is any evidence, however tenuous, from which the agreement might be inferred, the acts and words of any of the alleged conspirators, alleged to have been done or spoken in pursuance of the conspiracy, are admissible in evidence against all the others, on the footing that they are all agents of one another (although, at the time when the evidence is admitted, the jury has not found that there was an agreement—and so some agency— as alleged).

It is easy to see how almost any joint action, peaceful or violent, by even a small number of people, for a political or any other purpose, can be charged as a conspiracy. Progressive judges, politicians and supporters of civil liberty in all countries applying the principles of English law have long protested against the use of charges of conspiracy to secure the conviction and imprisonment of persons against whom no specific offence could possibly be proved; but governments have continued to use this formidable and easy weapon in the class struggle.

The last of the common law offences which are frequently political in content, which I must consider before I turn to statutory crimes, is that of criminal libel. Libel—whether civil or criminal—can be roughly defined as the publication to any third party of words (or pictures) written or printed, which tend to blacken the character of anyone and thereby to bring him into hatred, contempt or ridicule. Words to the same effect, not written but spoken, are called "slander", and libel and slander are often grouped under the one label of "defamation".

Nowadays, defamation is nearly always treated by the person defamed as a tort, i.e., a civil wrong (I shall discuss both torts in general and defamation in particular in Book 4) and he seeks his remedy by bringing action in a civil Court against all or any of those who took part in the publication. But libel can be treated as a criminal offence if it is alleged to be couched in language likely to provoke a breach of the peace, or if it is a libel on a class or group of people, so expressed as not to identify any particular individual as a target, and thus not to give any individual a right to sue civilly. Prosecutions for criminal libel are rare today, particularly because the civil remedy, namely damages payable to the plaintiff, is highly attractive; but they are still brought occasionally, and were, and even still are, frequent in certain colonial or ex-colonial territories, especially in political cases.

Slander can be made the subject of criminal prosecution only if it tends quite directly to cause a breach of the peace; prosecutions for it are very rare indeed.

I now come to the various Acts of Parliament which can be classified as political. They normally operate by providing that this or that activity shall be a crime, and punishable as such; but the earliest in point of time is the curious statute of 1367, 34 Edw. III, c. 1. This Act laid down that the ·justices (i.e., as I explained in Chapter 8 of Book 2, the justices of the peace, who are today generally called magistrates) should have power to enquire about "all those that have been pillors and robbers in all the parts beyond the sea, and be now come again, and go wandering, and will not labour as they were wont in times past, and to take and arrest all those that they may find by indictment or by suspicion, and to put them in prison; and to take of all them that be (not)* of good fame, where they shall be found, sufficient surety and mainprise of their good behaviour

* As a result of uncertainty in the text, it is impossible to determine whether the word "not" should be part of the Act.

towards the King and his people, and the other duly to punish, to the intent that the people be not by such rioters or rebels troubled nor endamaged, not the peace blemished, nor merchants or other passing by the highways of the realm disturbed nor put in peril which may happen of such offenders". In the course of centuries, case law has gradually established that the magistrates may, under this statute, order any person to give security for his good behaviour, or in default to go to prison, although he has never been a "pillor or robber", and although he has never committed, and is not even alleged to have committed, any criminal offence, on the ground that it is suspected that he may be going to cause a breach of the peace, without even any apprehension of violence and without anyone being put in bodily fear.

It is possible that this museum piece of legislation may be repealed in the near future, but it is still law, and is not infrequently used. One striking example of its use—serving the desire of the government to "put away" working-class leaders at times of important political and economic trouble—occurred in December, 1932. "Hunger-marchers", suffering from the terrible and long-drawn-out mass unemployment of that period, were arriving in London, and it was desired that a deputation should be received by the Prime Minister on the 19th December to present a petition, and should also be allowed to state their views to the House of Commons It might be thought that there was nothing very terrible or criminal in that, but nevertheless the working-class leader, Tom Mann (already briefly mentioned earlier in this chapter, and the victorious accused in the famous sedition prosecution—arising out of a similar "Hunger-march" situation—which will be related in Chapter 4) was arrested on the 16th December (yes, arrested) and brought before a magistrate as "a disturber of the peace and an inciter of persons to take part in mass demonstrations which are calculated to involve . . . contraventions of the provisions of the Seditious Meetings Act, 1817, and as such are subject to the provisions of the statute of 34 Edw. III, c. 1". (The Act of 1817, one of Lord Sidmouth's "Gagging Acts", prohibits the calling or holding of any meeting of more than fifty persons anywhere within one mile of Westminster Hall "for the purpose or on the pretext of considering of or preparing any petition . . . to . . . either House of Parliament for alteration of matters in Church or State".)

The prosecution—if one may loosely call it so, for no crime was or needed to be alleged under the 1367 statute—based its demand for Mann to be bound over on its assertion that, if a mass meeting were held, there might be violence. It was a thin case, even under that statute, and the evidence used to implicate Mann in the calling of the proposed meeting was both weak and largely inadmissible in law; but the magistrate ordered Mann to give surety "to keep the peace and be of good behaviour for twelve months", or in default to go to prison for two months. Mann was not the sort of person to give such surety, so he went to prison, at a time when there was vital work for him to do, not merely without having been convicted of a crime but without even being accused of one. (And the government served its own dirty purpose by thus eliminating for a time an important fighter for working-class rights at an important period.)

The next Acts of Parliament to be considered came around the end of the eighteenth century. The first of them is the Incitement to Mutiny Act, 1797, passed under the influence of the excitement caused by the famous Mutiny at the Nore, at a time of considerable unrest, both international and industrial. It provides that everyone who maliciously and advisedly endeavours to seduce anyone serving in His Majesty's forces from his duty and allegiance, or who incites anyone so serving to commit any act of mutiny or to make any mutinous assembly or to commit any traitorous or mutinous practice, may be punishable with life imprisonment. With this Act, I should consider the Incitement to Disaffection Act, 1934, which looks rather like a "popular edition" of it. Introduced in the hard times of the 'thirties, not long after the imprisonment of Tom Mann just described, the 1934 Act was discreetly heralded in the government press as an unimportant measure, primarily aimed at the fascists; but in its original form it was so loose and wide in its terms that one would have thought that the government expected a revolution in the next few weeks. It had the remarkable effect of binding together the forces of Left and Centre in a united front of furious onslaught on the Bill. In spite of the tiny numbers of the opposition in Parliament at the time, the Bill was gradually whittled away until in its final form it was little worse than the Incitement to Mutiny Act. The only substantial advantage for the government was that it enabled it to prosecute in the police Courts, without going before a jury, people who, under the earlier Act, would have had to go before a jury. (The importance of this for reactionary governments was discussed at length in Chapter 9 of Book 2.)

I return to the eighteenth century to consider the Unlawful Oaths Act, 1797 (a cousin, so to speak, of the Incitement to Mutiny Act), and the Unlawful Societies Act, 1799. These two Acts were combined and used in the government conspiracy, as it may fairly be called, to "railroad"—more precisely, to transport to Australia—the famous Tolpuddle Martyrs for forming a trade union of agricultural workers. I described this case in detail in Chapter 2 of Book 1, and need not deal with it here, but I must state shortly the substance of the two Acts. The first of them made it a felony to take any part whatever in administering an oath purporting or intending to bind the person taking it to engage in any mutinous or seditious purpose, or a good many other things of a similar nature; and the second, passed under the scare of the French Revolution, and aimed largely against the "Corresponding Societies" which were agitating for parliamentary reform and for the recognition of Thomas Paine's "Rights of Man", provided that every society whose members were required to take an oath not authorised by law should be taken to be an unlawful combination.

There is then the Unlawful Drilling Act, 1819, which is still in force, like the others, and was indeed expressly amended by the Firearms Act, 1920. By this Act, which was one of the infamous "Six Acts" of 1819, all meetings and assemblies of persons for the purpose of training or drilling in the use of arms or practising military evolutions without lawful authority from the government, are made criminal.

Coming again to the 'thirties of the present century, we have the Public Order Act, 1936. By no means wholly bad, this Act nevertheless introduces a highly dangerous element into the law relating to public meetings. It was passed largely to deal with the fascist habit of wearing uniforms; but it also makes it an offence to take part in the control or management of any association whose members are "organised or trained or equipped" for the purpose of enabling them to be employed in usurping the functions of the police or of the armed forces of the Crown, or are "organised and trained or organised and equipped either for the purpose of enabling them to be employed for the use or display of physical force in promoting any political object, *or in such manner as to arouse reasonable apprehension that they are organised and either trained or equipped for that purpose*". To much of this, little objection might be taken, but when *agents provocateurs* (see the next chapter) can be employed, and police evidence of doubtful quality can be eagerly accepted in police Courts in times of tension, there is a good deal of danger in the Act.*

There is more dangerous matter in this Act. Again with the excuse of dealing with fascists, it empowers various police authorities, when they are of the opinion (which cannot be tested in the Courts) that they cannot otherwise prevent disorder, to prohibit all public processions for up to three months in the whole or any part of their district. Processions, often called "demonstrations", are an important part of working-class political life, and such a prohibition, which can be laid upon everybody, including all working-class organisations, at the uncontrolled decision of the police, perhaps because fascists have deliberately created an atmosphere of potential disorder, is really intolerable.

I should next deal with the Emergency Powers Act, 1920, which was passed "to make exceptional provision for the protection of the community in cases of emergency". Shortly, the Act provides that at any time, if the government thinks (and the Courts cannot enquire into the ground or absence of ground for its thought) "that any action has been taken or is immediately threatened by any persons or body of persons of such a nature and on so extensive a scale as to be calculated, by interfering with the supply and distribution of food, water, fuel or light, or with the means of locomotion, to deprive the community or any substantial portion of the community of the essentials of life", then the government can "proclaim an

* When the Bill was brought in I had been a member of Parliament for only a few months, and I remember that when, after writing a strong condemnation of the Bill for the *New Statesman and Nation*, I went down to the House to attend the Second Reading debate on the Bill, I was astonished to find that the leaders of the Labour Party had decided to support it.

emergency". The proclamation is only valid for one month, but the state of emergency can be carried on indefinitely by a series of proclamations.

When an emergency has been proclaimed, what can the government do? The Act wraps up the answer in many words, but the short answer is that it can do anything it likes. It is empowered "to make regulations for securing the essentials of life to the community", and these regulations may confer or impose on any government department, *or on anyone acting for the government*, any power or duty that the government thinks necessary (and, again, the Courts will not enquire into the grounds for its thoughts) for the "preservation of the peace" (our old acquaintance "loranorder"), for securing and regulating the supply and distribution of food, water, fuel, light and other necessities, for maintaining the means of transit or locomotion, and for any other purposes essential to the public safety and the life of community (subject only to the reservation that the regulations are not to impose military or industrial conscription or to make it an offence to take part in a strike or peacefully to persuade others to do so). It does not require much imagination to see that any reactionary government in any time of industrial or political tension can if so minded—subject only to the pressure of public opinion, which on the one hand is potentially very powerful and on the other can be influenced by government bamboozlement—in due form of law and by using one sheet of paper a month, virtually do away with the whole protection of the existing law and the Courts, and establish a complete dictatorship.

Looking at all the mass of political law established in part by the common law and in part by statute, we can see that a pretty formidable collection of offences, very wide and dangerously vague in definition, lie in readiness for use at any moment of emergency, including in emergency the justified or unjustified fears of the ruling class that it may be in danger of losing power.

There are then the Official Secrets Acts. The first such Act still in force is that of 1911, (1 & 2, Geo. 5, c. 28), which was rushed through all its stages in the House of Commons in an hour, on the plea that it was needed to deal with "the German menace"; it was subsequently amended in 1920, 1939 and 1948.

This legislation lies on the fringe of my subject, for it is not primarily designed to serve the class struggle, but rather to deal with any activity, major or minor, falling within a wide definition of espionage. Most prosecutions under these Acts have been brought either against persons having access in the course of their duties to official information of a confidential nature, or against persons, British or foreign, alleged to be engaged in unlawful efforts to obtain such information. But the Acts have been used to hamper or to "frame" progressive persons or organisations, and in the unending war against Communists, or anyone who can plausibly be labelled Communist, it is not infrequent that some of them are accused of espionage. Demonstrations outside military aerodromes or other "prohibited places" have often been made the subject of prosecutions under these Acts, and one illustration of their use in political cases was given in Chapter 8 of Book 2, in the case of a civil servant who was prosecuted in Surrey.

The Acts, while they deal with matters that should certainly be covered by legislation, are extremely wide and sweeping in their terms—a defect which was made easier of achievement in the circumstances in which the first of them was rushed through Parliament in 1911; and they offend against many of the principles ordinarily applied to criminal legislation by going some way to making accused persons demonstrate their innocence and by compelling them to give information which may incriminate them.

I need not write in greater detail about the Official Secrets Acts here, for most attempts to hamper progressive activities are made under other Acts of Parliament or under the common law.

Finally, I must mention the various statutory provisions, referred to briefly above, which are used to hamper political activities—mainly meetings and demonstrations—by prosecutions in the police Courts, quick and easy from the police point of view, involving no jury trial, and leading generally to fines, often heavy ones, and to short or not very short terms of imprisonment. These "policeman's friend" sections enable people to be charged with such offences as obstructing the traffic, obstructing the police in the execution of their duty, assault, and "using insulting words and behaviour".

2

The Conduct of Political Prosecutions

In studying political prosecutions, one should not confine oneself to what takes place in Court when a case has once been launched, but should also consider the work of deciding what prosecutions should be brought against what persons, and on what charges, how evidence should be obtained, what witnesses should actually be called, and how honestly they should behave in the witness-box. The trial itself has also to be considered: how it should be conducted, with what regard for propriety, and how the accused and his witnesses should be cross-examined.

Our law is pretty full of ostensible safeguards for those who are or may be accused of crimes; for example, they are not bound to answer questions put to them by the police investigators, they have to be told at a certain stage of the investigation that they are not so bound—actually at the moment when the police make up their minds to charge them (a moment which, after all, can be fixed by the police themselves, at a conveniently late stage, since their minds are made up silently, by themselves). Again, evidence of the bad character or previous convictions of the accused must not be mentioned before the verdict is given (subject to certain exceptions, all of which are, so to speak, provoked by the accused himself). There is also a valuable provision that, in all major cases (i.e., those which are not finally disposed of in the police Courts but are sent by them, after a preliminary investigation, to Quarter Sessions or Assizes to be tried before a jury), the accused shall have full knowledge in advance of the prosecution evidence he will have to meet. Of this he must be informed not just by a bald statement in the indictment (the formal written charge which initiates every major trial) but by the witnesses being called before the magistrates and submitted for cross-examination in his presence (or, under recent legislation, there must be put before him at the same stage at least full written statements).

Perhaps even more important is the principle that—subject to statutory exceptions in certain narrowly-defined circumstances—every accused person is deemed innocent until he is proved guilty—in more lawyerly terms, that the burden of proof rests on the prosecution—and further that no one should be convicted just on the balance of probabilities, but that his guilt should be established to the satisfaction of the jury "beyond reasonable doubt"—an ambiguous phrase, but one which works out fairly well in practice. In addition, the law of evidence, stated shortly and broadly, lays down that every fact must be proved by first-hand direct evidence, and not by hearsay, and that the evidence should be confined to proof of what the accused himself (or his agent authorised by him to act for him under circumstances making it reasonable to employ the agent for this purpose) said or did, or what was said or done in his hearing or presence (or, in the case of such things as letters, received and read by him).

All these provisions, if fairly observed, are substantial; and there is a further if less precisely definable safeguard in the convention that counsel for the prosecution, or the solicitors or police prosecutors who conduct minor cases, must act fairly in the conduct of a case in Court, and must not call witnesses whom they know to be untrustworthy (they are said to "vouch" every witness they call as reliable) or—in cases where they have to call witnesses of bad character, perhaps accomplices of the accused—they must frankly tell the Court of this, and have corroboration for such witnesses if possible.

Safeguards are of no use if they are not observed reasonably well, and it must be admitted that in general, in cases with no elements of politics in them, those which I have just described are observed well enough, particularly in open Court. But there is nevertheless, at the various stages at which they come into play, and with people of varying standards and qualifications coming into the work at these various stages, a certain amount of unsatisfactory conduct even in non-political cases. (I shall have to give some account of this, but it will be more convenient not to do so at this stage, but wait until I come to state what happens in political cases, and then deal with the whole matter once and for all.)

The general picture becomes wholly different as soon as one moves into the political field. I remember that, when I was undertaking one of my early political defences at the Central Criminal Court, the late W. H. Thompson, the great left-wing solicitor of whom I have already written, said to me:

"Look here, Pritt, you know how to conduct a case, but you haven't the least idea what you have to put up with in the way of dirty tricks from the judge and the prosecution in a political case. You'll smell the hostility the moment you go through the door of the Court, and you'll do more than just smell it as soon as the hearing starts, and all the way through!"

I did not for the moment wholly accept this, and told him so. He replied: "All right, wait and see." I did not have to wait long, and I saw so much, both in that case and in countless others which followed it, that I began to wonder why I had ever for a moment doubted him. There is really no limit to the departures from fair dealing which one has to expect from the police and the prosecution, and often too from the judges, in political cases. I will describe some of the cases in Chapters 4 and 8, the first devoted to illustrations in England, and the second to those in the colonies. But I should give at once some details of the types of breaches of the safeguards committed, dealing as I promised both with political and non-political cases; naturally, these occur most frequently under circumstances where it is not easy to check on them at the time, or sometimes even later. I will take them in the order in which they arise, chronologically, from the progress of an offence, and will point out, where necessary, the differences between political and non-political cases.

I begin with the earliest stage, when the offence, if it was really committed, was being prepared, and when, sometimes, it was being instigated by *agents provocateurs*, or invented by perjurers "out of whole cloth". This happens, of course, most frequently in political cases. The malpractices relative to this stage are various. The simplest is the deliberate concoction or invention of evidence to "prove" that some political accused has committed some crime or other when in fact no such crime ever took place—something more complete in its inventive wickedness than such malpractices as the case of Sacco and Vanzetti, where a crime had really been committed and the prosecution "only" sought to destroy progressive political leaders by implicating them in it when in fact they had had nothing to do with it.

The second of these malpractices, in some ways even worse than the first, is the employment of *agents provocateurs* to incite men burdened with grievances to go beyond peaceful protests and do something which can be charged as criminal (and much can be charged as criminal under such laws as that of conspiracy, discussed in the previous chapter), and then to denounce them.

The third, a little milder than the second, is the employment of spies or paid informers to get information by one means or another of the possibly criminal activities of working-class politicians, and then to denounce them.

Alongside these three sorts of malpractice I will consider the use of accomplice evidence, not in itself a malpractice, but lending itself to similar abuses. I will deal with these four varieties of malpractice and give some illustrations.

On the first class, that of stories invented "out of whole cloth", it may be difficult for some people to believe that this happens, but I can give several examples from my own experience. The crudest example, particularly clearly proved—for it was subsequently admitted on oath by the inventor—was that of the star witness called against Jomo Kenyatta on his trial which I describe below, in Chapter 8. The inventor-witness was paid, "in meal or in malt", over £2,500 by the Kenya government for giving "evidence" on oath of alleged "Mau Mau" activities of Kenyatta, none of which had ever taken place at all.

My next example comes from the Telengana cases, tried in India in and around 1950. A group of young and courageous rebellious peasants in what is now the State of Andhra and was then part of the Prince's State of Hyderabad, took over the land from the rich landlords and distributed it among the poor peasants. When this operation was finally crushed by the Indian army, a number of these men were framed on all sorts of charges—including murder—which were demonstrably untrue and had been invented simply as an effective means of taking vengeance on the rebels. (It was a long and disgraceful story, which space does not permit me to describe fully here; it is dealt with fully in Chapter 3 of the third volume of my *Autobiography*, "The Defence Accuses".)

There are more examples in the long and hitherto unsuccessful efforts of the United States government to destroy the militant Australian Harry Bridges, leader of a strong trade union on the Pacific Coast of the U.S.; one of these examples came to my personal knowledge, as I was able to help Bridges obtain proof of the invention practised against him. An informer or purported informer gave evidence before the notorious "Dies" Committee of the House of Representatives to the effect that he had seen Bridges attending, as a member, various Communist Party meetings in California. When this informer had left the U.S. and returned to his native Scotland, he swore an affidavit to the effect that he had been compelled to invent this story and give evidence of it by threats that if he did not do so he would be prosecuted for non-political crimes which, to the knowledge of the U.S. government, he had in fact committed. I had long talks with him in London and in Scotland, and I was convinced that his affidavit contained the truth.

In the second class, of which I gave long accounts involving both this country and the U.S. in my book *Spies and Informers in the Witness Box*, published in 1958, the worst period in English history was the early part of the nineteenth century, a period of industrial and political unrest; much of the story is well told in the books of J. L. and Barbara Hammond, *The Town Labourer, 1760–1832*, and *The Skilled Labourer, 1760–1832*. The most notorious of the *agents provocateurs* who did an infinite amount of damage, was one Oliver, employed and paid by the Home Office. It might have been thought that in more modern times the British government has ceased to resort to such measures—except that it is always a mistake to imagine that there is any limit to such a government's villainy in the class struggle—but the disquieting Wheeldon case, tried in 1917 during the First World War, is some contradiction of this happy idea. A Mrs. Wheeldon, her two daughters, and her son-in-law were prosecuted for conspiracy to murder the Prime

Minister (David Lloyd George) and one of his Ministers (Arthur Henderson), and for soliciting one Booth to murder them. Mrs. Wheeldon had political affiliations that were unwelcome to the government, although not illegal, and was very active in helping conscientious objectors to military service who were "on the run". When it came to a question of murder, however, the only evidence that could implicate any of the accused was that of spies set on them by the government; and a still worse feature was that one spy, a man using the name of Gordon, who was indeed an *agent provocateur*, and was deeply involved in whatever was in truth happening, was not called as a witness in spite of persistent pressure from the accused. (There was a strong suspicion that he was a man who had himself been convicted of a cold-blooded murder.) His absence from the witness-box left the evidence of Mrs. Wheeldon uncontradicted; the only serious fact adduced·against the accused was that they had obtained a supply of poison, and Mrs. Wheeldon's uncontradicted evidence was that Gordon, who professed to be helping conscientious objectors, had asked her to get it for no more sinister purpose than to kill dogs that were guarding camps where these objectors were detained. Nevertheless, the accused were convicted and sentenced to long terms of imprisonment.

In dealing with the third class, that of informers, I must be careful not wholly to condemn the use of informers, for much non-political and anti-social criminal activity would remain unpunished if the police were not able to get information from informers as to who had been guilty of crimes that were under investigation, and then go on to find reliable evidence on which to prosecute. It is to the use of informers *as witnesses* that one should object strongly; hence the title of my book *Spies and Informers in the Witness Box*. Informers, especially those who are regularly employed and paid, are often people of little scruple, and know that the more "helpful" their evidence is to those who pay them the more money they will earn. It is very easy for them to embroider their evidence so as to make it more helpful, often by telling a story which is in the main true but is embroidered by such "helpful" falsehoods as that the accused was present when he was not. The use of professional and highly-paid informers as witnesses in scores and scores of cases is common in the U.S.A., especially, of course, in political cases; and it is not unknown here.

As for accomplices, it is not—as I have said—a malpractice to call them as witnesses, but it is easily liable to abuse. Participants in crime who "turn Queen's evidence" and go into the witness-box to swear away the liberty and perhaps the lives of those with whom they have acted are treated in law as witnesses where evidence should very seldom be accepted unless it is corroborated by untainted witnesses. An accomplice who has been pardoned, so that he has nothing to fear directly in the way of punishment for his share in the alleged crime, is no more untrustworthy than anyone else who is prepared to betray his comrades; but one who has neither been pardoned nor tried, convicted and sentenced has plainly the grave additional defect that he must know and feel that the risk of his going to prison (and the length of his possible sentence) will diminish in proportion to the amount of help his evidence gives to the prosecution. And even one who has been sentenced must feel that he has a chance of being released long before he has served his complete sentence, on the same footing. One of the worst instances of accomplice evidence given under temptation of this sort came in the notorious prosecution in New York of Ethel and Julius Rosenberg in 1950; the Rosenbergs could not have been convicted without the evidence of one Greenglass, a self-confessed accomplice, who at the time when he gave evidence was awaiting his own trial.

Examples of accomplice evidence in this country are to be found in my book mentioned above; and in the long court martial proceedings against Attwood and others in what was then British India at the end of the Second World War, which I describe below, in Chapter 4 (and, at length, in Volume 2, Chapter 11 of my *Autobiography*, "Brasshats and Bureaucrats", where one can read an elaboration of the investigators' trick of working hard to break down one or two of a group of potential accused in order to use them as witnesses against the other accused).

So much for a first stage of malpractices, which starts at the very beginning of an investigation, before those who are or may in the end be accused have even been questioned. The next stage comes, still before any arrest or charge, when the police are questioning people who may be able to give information, whether or not they are likely themselves to be accused. Here the main faults of the police lie in long-drawn-out and severe questioning ("helping the police in their enquiries"), in laying traps for a suspect—often, for example, falsely telling each member of a group, questioned separately, that one or more of the others have confessed—in obstructing requests to communicate with their family or their solicitor, and in not informing them that they have a right to refuse to answer questions. Everyone knows that this sort of thing happens; but no one can say with confidence to how great an extent; and one of the difficulties of finding out is the fact that, after all, a good many of the people questioned by the police, especially in non-political cases, are persons of bad character, not necessarily to be believed when they allege some misbehaviour by the questioners.

The next stage comes after arrest or charge; the faults that are sometimes committed here by the police will be much the same as those of the previous stage, with the important exceptions of the beating-up of accused persons to extract confessions and the planting of such things as offensive weapons on them. Beating-up, again, is one of the things that everyone knows happen, though no one can really tell to what extent. There was some very disquieting evidence a few years ago of the practice being rife in Sheffield, and—as I recorded at pp. 173-4 of "Brasshats and Bureaucrats"—the practice has been admitted to me by a high official of Scotland Yard. This is a field in which there may be some difference between political and non-political cases; on the one hand, beating-up is a little more likely when the authorities are particularly anxious to secure a conviction, and on the other the police will be more careful when dealing with intelligent and articulate persons who are likely to take steps, such as having themselves independently medically examined at the earliest possible moment, and suing the police in the civil Courts for damages for assault.

As for the planting of evidence, here again it is not easy to ascertain with any surety to what extent the practice prevails. There were some startling revelations in London a few years ago to the effect that one high officer was "planting" regularly, and instructing his subordinates to do the same; investigation led to the disquieting but possibly true explanation being given that the official involved had in fact been insane for a long time without his colleagues noticing this normally obvious defect.

A pretty serious malpractice, which has developed in recent years in line with the increase in political demonstrations, is to be found in the practice of selecting what persons should be arrested in a crowd, together with the perjury often involved on the part of police witnesses who give evidence against the accused so selected. I am not referring to the practice of police witnesses, who know that the magistrates will almost certainly accept their evidence, swearing that a particular accused did something which was done by somebody else in the course of the demonstration, but to a more organised system, of which there has been substantial evidence in connection with recent political demonstrations. Every big demonstration is, naturally enough, attended by a number of "Special Branch" men in plain clothes, who will recognise among the demonstrators some politically active people who would naturally and lawfully attend such an event. From the point of view of the police, it is important to secure convictions of such people rather than of the general mass, for they can thus hamper and weaken the serious progressive elements, perhaps scare a few of them off demonstrations altogether, cause them expense, and get some of them labelled as "previously convicted" so as to get them heavier fines or even imprisonment when they take part in subsequent demonstrations. In this way the police may hope gradually to cripple demonstrations generally. The Special Branch men do not want to give evidence in Court themselves, for they would then become known (technically, "blown") and much of their value in their semi-espionage profession would thus be lost. In order both to secure convictions and to keep the Special Branch men from becoming known, a pretty disgraceful manœuvre is used. In a typical demonstration, there will be a certain number of uniformed police and a certain number of Special Branch men, known to the uniformed men but not —as they hope—to the general body of demonstrators. The Special Branch men will unostentatiously signal (fingering) to the uniformed men this or that person whom the former recognise as "political", and the uniformed men will then

arrest them. Then the problem of keeping the Special Branch
men out of the witness-box is solved by their telling the uniformed men what they saw, or say that they saw, the arrested
men doing, and by the uniformed men then going into the
witness-box and swearing that they themselves saw all these
alleged acts being done by the accused (perjury). It may
startle some people to learn that the police thus commit
perjury. But I have the authority of the high police officer
whom I have already quoted for the practice of the police
committing perjury to secure the conviction of persons who,
they are sure, have committed the offence charged against
them. And it is a very short step from that to this new practice,
aided by the knowledge that the magistrates will accept police
evidence.

This brings me to the stage of the proceedings where the trial
takes place in open Court. Here, as I said earlier, behaviour is
in general better. But in political cases there are still marked
departures from proper behaviour, of which I will give examples
in Chapter 4; as we shall see in Part 2 of this book the position
in the Colonies has generally been far worse. But I must still
write something of the matter here.

In major cases, the judge is often involved in malpractices,
as well as the prosecuting counsel. Consciously or uncon-
sciously, the judge will lean against political accused in many
ways, e.g., on questions of granting bail, in ruling on questions
of the admissibility of evidence or on other points of law,*
in interrupting the accused and his counsel with warnings
that they "must not talk politics" when in reality they are
doing no more than making their defence, in which of course
politics are vitally involved (he might as well tell people not to

---

* In a political case in which I took part in the defence in Düsseldorf in 1959–60,
the rulings against the admissibility of evidence went to such extremes that one of
the German counsel engaged in the case boldly said to the Court:

"You are preventing a real determination as to whether the accused or any of
them have in fact broken the law, because you reject evidence which goes to the
very core of the case. I tell you frankly, I have the impression that it would be
better not to hold these trials by judicial procedure, but just to proceed administratively and lock up our clients in a camp. . . .

"What are we defence counsel to do? Are we to sit here in our robes, as part of
the setting of the frame-up? In other criminal cases, having no special political
background, such rulings would be simply impossible. . . .

"If you tell us that it is enough that four of the (six) accused were members
of the Communist Party, then the matter is clear, and we need make no more
applications to adduce evidence."

talk music in a case which turns on music), and above all in his
summing up to the jury, all of which may have a great influence
on the result. And the magistrates who deal with minor cases,
as I explained at length in Book 2, Chapter 8, will behave rather
worse.

And, in any political case, one of the common prosecution
tricks is to ask the accused in cross-examination whether he is a
Communist. An accused person may in general be asked only
questions which tend to prove that he is guilty of the offence
charged, and such a question about membership of a political
party should not be asked; but once it is asked the damage is
done by the mere asking, whether the question be disallowed or
not, and whatever answer is given to it.

3

The Defence in Political Prosecutions

The problems of the defence in political cases are very different from those which I discussed in the previous chapter. The defence has no opportunity, and in general little desire, to indulge in malpractices, although it will naturally fight hard and "give nothing away". But there are many differences between the conduct of defences as between political and non-political cases, especially for the advocates. The differences begin, indeed, when the advocates are being chosen for any particular case. In ordinary practice, a barrister or a solicitor appears for anyone who seeks to employ him, regardless of his own views, convictions and sympathies, of the merits or demerits of the case or the client, and of the social, political or economic results; if it were not so, many accused would have difficulty in securing a defence. The defending counsel will have no regard, indeed, for anything but his duty to present cases with all proper vigour, with a view to winning them for his clients by legitimate means; it does not matter to the advocate (apart from the human pleasure of winning, and the desire to build up a reputation and a practice) which side wins, or how socially or even personally healthy or disastrous the result may be.

But when it comes to political cases, there are very different problems, not only as to how the case should be fought, but also as to how barristers or solicitors should be selected to conduct the case, and as to whether they accept it. It has become increasingly difficult, as world tensions increase and politics become more complicated, for an advocate to represent a political defendant effectively unless he sympathises with his outlook, or at least fully understands it. At times this makes it difficult for political defendants to find advocates to conduct their cases. It is in theory a rule of our professional etiquette that barristers are bound to accept and conduct any case which falls within the general scope of their practice, whether they sympathise with their client's views or not. In the eighteenth and early nineteenth centuries many political accused were well defended by some of the finest advocates of the time, and the system did not work too badly; barristers of middle- or upper-middle-class outlook seemed able to understand, even if they did not sympathise with, the motives that had influenced many people accused of riot, or sedition, or treason, and could defend them with vigour and sincerity. But in the last fifty years or more the gulf in ideas between those—Communists or Left-Wing Labour people or at times pacifists—who are likely to be accused in political cases and the ordinary run of barristers has become so wide that it is now really impossible for the bulk of the latter to understand the background of such cases sufficiently well to defend them adequately. Moreover, those likely to be accused in such cases have generally no confidence that they can be adequately defended by any barrister who is not pretty near to their own point of view. The old rule of etiquette, which is in any case fairly easily evaded by anyone who does not want to take a case, has thus become of little practical value; and the need for politically progressive lawyers to conduct such cases is met by the existence of a small group —barely sufficient—of barristers and solicitors who can really work whole-heartedly and with full understanding for political accused.

Another differentiating feature of political cases that is difficult for lawyers to understand at first sight is that the primary object of a good political defence is not to win the case—although victory, if it should perchance come, is very welcome and useful—but to maintain and propagate the client's political point of view. One must never sacrifice or compromise principles for the sake of winning (or even of securing a shorter sentence). Such a defence as: "My client is a young man who was carried away by his enthusiasm; he now knows better, and will not do such a thing again", is quite inadmissible. It is vital to justify the accused's action politically—and the policy and conduct of his party if he belongs to one—and if possible to go further and to turn defence into counter-attack, denouncing and discrediting the government both for prosecuting for political reasons and for pursuing the bad policies which led the accused to react as he did; and, moreover, to do all this with as much publicity as possible. Let victory come, certainly, if it can, as a result of these efforts, so long as there is no sacrifice of principle; but these efforts are the essential thing, and a real political victory is won even if the case itself is lost, so long as the principles and policies of the government and of the accused and his party are displayed in their true light. (At times such victories are very great; I have seen and experienced several outwardly "successful" political prosecutions which made the intolerant and intransigent attitude of a colonial government so clear to the mass of the people that the independence of the territory conceived was brought about some years sooner than was expected.)

The duty of the barrister to do his best for his client is as strong in political cases as in others—it could not be stronger, for one must always do one's best; but doing one's "best" in a political case is not to secure victory by any sacrifice of principle, and one's duty has to be performed in a different way and with a different object.

Another interesting feature of political cases is that nearly every case is not just one case but in reality any number up to several hundred. By this I mean that, if a case is not fought, and fought hard and politically, the government concerned, U.K. or colonial, will launch many more similar cases. Sometimes this happens because the government, having launched the one case and found that little public indignation has been aroused, is tempted to try again; "l'appetit vient en mangeant". And sometimes a government whilst it is anxious to hamper popular oppositon, and eager to cripple a whole string of its opponents by getting them convicted and sentenced, will see the danger of bringing a large number of cases at once, lest it lose them all. It therefore starts with one or two cases to see "how it works". If it both gets convictions and excites little public indignation, it will launch a further series of cases. But if things go badly for it, it will drop the further cases, and thereby lose only a little face, for the public may not even know that it had planned further cases. There are one or two well-known instances where it was pretty plain that a series of prosecutions had been planned, but had to be dropped when the first one, the "trial run", came to grief. For example, at the time of the famous "Reichstag Fire" trial at Leipzig in 1933, staged by the Nazis as an attempt to discredit the Communist Party, and turned by the genius of the principal accused, Georgi Dimitrov, into a tremendous defeat for the Nazis, it was generally believed that a number of further political trials, with the maximum of publicity on the lines used in the early stages of the Leipzig case, had been planned. But after the defeat in that case the Nazis, although in the years of horror that were to follow they tried innumerable people in "Special Courts" and executed them in scores of thousands, never attempted to stage anything in the nature of a "state trial" of any important person. Another instance, not a typical one, for no trial was ever held, but a good illustration of the way in which public opinion when roused can put a stop to political trials, came in the case of the Cairo Forces Parliament, described in Chapter 6 of the second volume of my *Autobiography*, "Brasshats and Bureaucrats". In that case the British military authorities in Egypt, in the early part of 1944, behaved with incredible stupidity, and made many attempts to stifle critics by such steps as "posting" them to distant and unpleasant stations where there was nothing for them to do. In spite of the authorities' best efforts, news of their activities was got through to myself and one or two other Members of Parliament, as a result of which their follies were brought to a stop. I thought at the time that, whilst we had just managed to stop them, we had not achieved very much; but after the war the principal worker in the admirable Cairo Forces Parliament which the military authorities had tried to destroy, one Leo Abse, now himself a Member of Parliament, called to thank me for my part in what he described as a "great victory". I asked him why it merited that description, and he replied that, at the time we had managed to raise the whole matter in Parliament, the Cairo "Blimps" were plotting a whole series of "postings" and other forms of revenge or punishment on the men who had been active in the Forces Parliament, and had had hurriedly to abandon their plans as soon as we in London had been able to arouse public opinion. In British Guiana, as it then was, there was another example. Two not very important members of the People's Progressive Party, the leading political organisation which was then laying the foundations of independence, were prosecuted for sedition, and—as described in Chapter 10 of *The Defence Accuses*—I went out to defend them, and they were acquitted. I learnt shortly afterwards that the colonial government had been planning a long series of such prosecutions, involving the highest leaders of the party, and had selected two relatively minor figures for the "trial run" as a prudent insurance against too much loss of face. No further cases were brought.

I add in conclusion the thought that, for lawyers who have political views, the opportunity and the duty of defending in political cases transforms their work into a sort of mission and a pleasure; for they are serving the interests of some of the best of their fellow-citizens, and the true interests of their country, whilst carrying on their profession (and perhaps actually earning their daily bread).

4

Some Illustrative Cases

In this chapter I give accounts of a number of cases which illustrate the various points I have made in earlier chapters about the manner—often the very unsatisfactory manner—in which political cases work out in practice. I shall confine myself for the moment to English cases (including court martial cases concerning British forces serving abroad), and one case in Quebec, leaving colonial cases to be dealt with later, in Chapter 8, which will come after I have described in Chapters 5 to 7 the features of our law as applied in the Colonies.

I take as my first illustration the case of *Liversidge* v. *Anderson*, decided by the House of Lords in November, 1941, and reported in the Law Reports, (1942) A.C. 206. It was free of the particular faults I have described in earlier chapters, for no evidence was involved at any stage of the case, and no malpractice could occur in the preparation of the case. The decision turned solely on the interpretation of a few words in a Defence Regulation, and everyone, counsel and judges alike, behaved with great propriety, at least until after the judgment had been given.

It was a very important case, concerning the liberty of the subject and the extent to which it might be right to interfere therewith in war-time, and it excited a great deal of public interest. It showed how far eminent judges would go in the government interest in war-time, by way of adopting what most people would regard as strange interpretations of words. One must remember that the same judges might at any time have to deal with words interfering with the liberty and rights not of external enemies but of persons on one side in the class war.

The case concerned the power of the Home Secretary under Defence Regulation 18B to intern people without charge or trial for an indefinite period. No supporter of civil liberties, and few other people, would at first sight approve of such a provision, but circumstances may clearly arise in war-time which make it necessary to intern people on the basis of information in the possession of the government, although it may be impossible either to prove them guilty of a criminal offence, or to disclose—without damage to the war effort—either the information in question or the source of it. What is essential is to guard as far as possible against abuse of the procedure, and to give the interned people information as to the grounds of their internment, and some opportunity for review of their cases.

Liversidge, the plaintiff and appellant, was interned under an Order made by the Home Secretary, Sir John Anderson, under the Regulation mentioned, which provided that when a Secretary of State (in practice the Home Secretary) had *reasonable cause* (my italics) to believe any person to be (among other things) of hostile associations, and that by reason thereof it was necessary to exercise control over him, the Secretary of State could make an internment order. The history of the drafting of the Regulation is a little complicated, and did not come up for discussion in the case, which turned on the correct interpretation of the words, quoted above, that actually appear in the Regulation; (it is a firm rule of interpretation in English law that the Court should not enquire into how the words arrived in the document involved, but should merely look at them as they are and determine their meaning). That did not of course mean that one could not criticise the drafting, which had led to a good deal of rather inconclusive litigation before Liversidge, under my advice, brought his action in such a form that it could be definitely determined, if necessary by the House of Lords.

When any statute or statutory Regulation empowers the Government to interfere with the rights of citizens to their liberty or any other important right, one matter which has to be determined is whether the Courts are to be allowed to examine and control acts done or purported to be done in exercise of the power. Such Regulations as 18b ought to be so drafted as to show clearly whether the decision of the Home Secretary can or cannot be challenged in the Courts. In the view which I put before the Courts on behalf of Liversidge, this had been done, and done in his favour. One of the usual formulae employed to exclude the Courts from jurisdiction in such matters is: "If the Secretary of State is satisfied that . . .", and another to the same effect runs: "If it appears to the Secretary of State that . . .". Another common formula, the one in fact used in 18B, is: "If the Secretary of State has reasonable cause to believe that . . .". This would normally imply the exact opposite; there was and is ample legal authority for the proposition that whenever anyone, however eminent, is given power to do some act *if* he has reasonable cause to believe something, the Courts—whose jurisdiction is not lightly to be excluded—are entitled to decide whether the cause which has made the Home Secretary, or whoever it may be, believe something was or was not a reasonable cause; if the Court decides that it was not reasonable, the detention is illegal, the man would have to be released, and the government could then make a better-drafted Regulation.

The way in which I advised Liversidge to sue need not be stated here; it was one which made it inevitable that the Courts must decide the crucial question which I have stated. We sued on that footing, lost in the High Court and in the Court of Appeal, and lost again in the House of Lords, where one very great judge, Lord Atkin, dissented from the other judges. His judgment, which became a very famous one, was to the effect that the Courts could test the "cause", as I had argued; the other four judges found one reason or another for ruling that the meaning of the Regulation was that when the Home Secretary, in good faith, made an internment order in which he stated that he had reasonable cause, the Court could not enquire whether his cause was reasonable.

It is worth quoting parts of Lord Atkin's judgment. He said that the case raised

"the issue as to the nature and limits of the authority of the Secretary of State to make orders that persons be detained under Regulation 18B of the Defence (General) Regulations, 1939. The matter is one of great importance both because the power to make orders is necessary for the defence of the realm, and because the liberty of the subject is seriously infringed, for the order does not purport to be made for the commission of an offence against the criminal law. It is made by an executive minister and not by any kind of judicial officer, it is not made after any inquiry as to facts to which the subject is party, it cannot be reversed on any appeal, and there is no limit to the period for which the detention may last."

Lord Atkin put the question of interpretation neatly a little later in his judgment, when he said that the argument which the majority of the House of Lords was accepting was that "the words 'if the Secretary of State has reasonable cause' merely mean 'if the Secretary of State thinks that he has reasonable cause' ".

One rather unusual reason for the increase of public interest in the case arose from some communications between the judges, partly made public, after their judgments had been prepared, and in part after they had been delivered; these are well-described in an article by Professor R. F. V. Heuston in the *Law Quarterly Review* of January, 1970. Lord Atkin's judgement was certainly vigorously expressed. It made plain —and indeed some of his observations in the course of the arguments had made plain—that he felt very strongly on the matter, and he drafted his judgment in the knowledge that all the other judges were going to hold that the Regulation meant that the Courts had no right to exercise any control over the use of the Home Secretary's power. These communications fell below the high standards which are expected of the judges, and might have been due to some extent to an uneasy conscience of those who felt that they were deciding in the interests of the government something which they knew not to be good law. The whole story is well told by Professor Heuston in the article mentioned.

I quote some more passages from Lord Atkin's judgment:

"It has always been one of the pillars of freedom, one of the principles of liberty for which on recent authority we are now fighting, that the judges are no respecters of persons and stand between the subject and any attempted encroachments on his liberty by the executive, alert to see that any coercive action is justified in law. In this case I have listened to arguments which might have been addressed acceptably to the Court of King's Bench in the time of Charles I. . . .

"The words (in the Regulation) have only one meaning. They are used with that meaning in statements of the common law and in statutes. They have never been used in the sense now imputed to them. There is no absurdity or no such degree of public mischief as would lead to a non-natural construction.

"I know of only one authority which might justify the suggested method of construction. 'When I use a word', Humpty Dumpty said in rather a scornful tone, 'it means just what I choose it to mean, neither more or less.' 'The question is', said Alice, 'whether you can make words mean different things.' The question is', said Humpty Dumpty, 'which is to be master, that's all.' "

Before the judgments were delivered, Lord Simon, the Lord Chancellor, who had not sat on the hearing of the appeal but had been able to see the text of Lord Atkin's judgment, wrote to him, asking him to omit the reference to Humpty Dumpty, as it might be regarded as wounding to the other judges who had sat. Lord Atkin replied, firmly but courteously, that he could not do so, and he delivered his judgment in the form in which he had drafted it. After the judgments, one or two other judges—who had not sat to hear the case—wrote privately to Lord Atkin with mild criticisms. Lord Maugham, however, who had sat on the case and taken a strong line the other way to Lord Atkin, wrote a letter to *The Times* attacking Lord Atkin for having said that he had listened to "arguments which might have been addressed acceptably to the Court of King's Bench in the time of Charles I", which Lord Maugham treated as a "grave animadversion" on the counsel who had appeared for the Home Secretary. It had not occurred to me at any stage of the proceedings that the counsel in question had done anything improper, nor indeed that Lord Atkin was suggesting in his judgment that they had done so. Lord Atkin did not reply in *The Times*, nor did I expect that he would. I wrote him a note offering to do so if he thought it would be helpful; at the same time various other barristers did write, and a leading article in the *Daily Telegraph* carried some criticism of Lord Maugham for his action. The matter was shortly afterwards discussed rather inconclusively in the House of Lords.

I need write nothing more here about the case itself, but I should write a little about the importance of proper observance of safeguards for the internees. The reasons which had to be and were given by the Home Office to Liversidge for his internment were not relevant to the argument before the House of Lords, and were not in fact mentioned; but they were brought privately to my knowledge. They were about as inadequate and disgraceful as could be imagined, considered as reasons given by a government department for the decision of its political head (who, according to what the government put forward in defence of 18B, made all the decisions himself, on his personal study of the cases) to deprive a citizen indefinitely of his liberty without charge or trial. The "reasons" ran roughly as follows:

"1. You are suspected of having been engaged in commercial frauds.

"2. You are suspected of having been in touch with persons who are suspected of being enemy agents.

"3. You are the son of a Jewish Rabbi."

The triviality of these reasons stands out as much as their bad moral quality. On the first of them, the fact was that my client had never even been charged with any criminal offence, and it is not easy to imagine how a suspected *commercial* fraud, which may never have been committed and in any case had led to no prosecution, could make a man a danger to the state; if, on a broad socialist point of view, it could be so held, my client should have been accompanied into internment by a number of "city gentlemen". The second reason had at least an air of having been connected with "security" matters; but it is noticeable that those who drafted this reason were not even prepared to say that Liversidge had actually been in touch with the suspected "agents", or that these people were actually enemy agents, still less that Liversidge knew that they were, *if* he were ever "in touch" with them. As for the third reason, those who put it forward were unfit to be in the service of the state at any time, and above all when we were engaged in a war against the anti-semitic Nazis. The only redeeming feature of the conduct of the Home Office is that it released Liversidge from internment shortly after the judgment.

By chance, I happened to learn of the "reasons" for the detention of one other victim of "18B". He was T. E. Nicholas, a famous Welsh poet, a Communist, and a dentist; it took a very long time for him even to get the "reasons", and when they finally reached him the least unsubstantial of them was the assertion that something had been painted at some time, by someone, on a bridge forming part of a public highway which he used once a week on his way to a surgery which he had in a small village near his home: that something was a swastika! He was released soon after his case had come before one of the tribunals which had been set up to examine cases of detention and to advise the Home Secretary—their powers were no more than advisory—whether the detainee should be released. The tribunal advised release, and Nicholas was soon released. But, like many other detainees, he had been waiting many months for a hearing.

If one were allowed to "generalise from a single instance"— or rather in this matter two instances—one would take a gloomy view of the administration of 18B; but no doubt many or most of the cases were genuine in the sense that the victims needed to be detained.

I next relate a case that was tried as long ago as 1925; it both illustrates vividly the shameless way in which our governments here—let alone what they were capable of doing in the colonies —will launch and conduct unjust and baseless prosecutions, and gives an even more startling picture of a ruling class closing its eyes to open and dangerous treason when the conspirators are members of itself.

In the autumn of 1925, the (Tory) government was alarmed at the prospect of an immediate general strike in support of a strike by coal-miners against their grossly inadequate wages and against the proposal of the mineowners to reduce those wages. The government was not then ready with its preparations to provide for the feeding of London during the general strike, and it in effect bought time to complete its preparations by giving the mineowners a subsidy to persuade them to continue paying the miners for six months their inadequate wages at the then inadequate scale. Having thus put itself in a

stronger position to fight the general strike when (and if)
it came six months later, the government conceived the idea of
strengthening itself further by crippling the small but efficient
and conscientious Communist Party by prosecuting, convicting
and imprisoning its leaders, so as to keep them out of circulation
during the period of preparation and of the actual strike (if it
should take place). If they could do this, they would have to
deal only with the T.U.C., whose (mostly right-wing) leaders
were very lukewarm about the whole idea of the strike, and
with the Labour Party, numerically large but not nearly
clear-headed and class-conscious enough to fight the government on such an issue.

Accordingly, in October, 1925, in a period of outward peace,
the government suddenly descended on the Communist Party
and the Young Communist League, which had been conducting
ordinary lawful political propaganda since their foundation
five years earlier with little interference from the government.
It prosecuted twelve leaders of the two organisations, basing
its case almost entirely on publications of ordinary political
propaganda. The charge in the police Court was formulated in
an allegation that the accused had been conspiring since the
12th January, 1924—the government thus accusing itself of
having idly watched a desperate conspiracy developing for
nearly two years—"to utter and publish seditious libels and to
incite divers persons to commit breaches of the Incitement to
Mutiny Act, 1797". (I dealt with this Act in a little detail in
Chapter 1, above.)

The government began by arresting the accused, and carrying away from their houses large quantities of their documents.
Such indiscriminate seizures were almost common form with
the "guardians of law and order" when dealing with Communists and other left-wingers, but they were generally illegal,
and in 1934, after a similar indiscriminate seizure of documents on the occasion of an arrest, several Communists recovered damages in the High Court against two police officers and
Lord Trenchard, the Commissioner of the Metropolitan Police.

The prosecution, crude and disgraceful in itself, was accompanied by all sorts of departures from normal behaviour,
which would never have been attempted or tolerated if the
accused had not been Communists, but were pretty typical of

political cases. For example, one Sir William Joynson-Hicks, a blustering second-rate solicitor who had "succeeded" in politics and become Home Secretary, indulged at the time of the arrests—i.e. long before any evidence had been given in the case, let alone the verdict—in what *The Times* described as "a most improper whoop", telling a public meeting in his constituency that warrants had been applied for against a number of "notorious Communists", and that several of them were already in custody. "When this trial is over," he said, "those of you who are Communists will be ashamed of yourselves." Any lawyer should have known that such an observation, which would be published in the press for all potential jurymen to read, was grossly improper; but Joynson-Hicks was not conspicuous for either discretion or legal knowledge.

On the 24th October, 1925, the case came on for its preliminary hearing in the police Court, where the opening speech of prosecuting counsel made the government's attitude plain. He bluntly asserted that the Communist Party and the Young Communist League were "illegal organisations", and that the accused were

> "all engaged in an illegal conspiracy, preaching the doctrines of what they call Communism. All persons," he said, "who disseminate either by word of mouth or by published writings the doctrines which these people call Communism are liable to be prosecuted for one or other of the branches of what is commonly called sedition—uttering seditious words or publishing seditious libels. Communism hails from Russia.
>
> "Communism is illegal because it involves three things: (1) the overthrow of the constituted government of the country and the established forms of government by force; (2) the creation of antagonism between different classes of His Majesty's subjects—'class-war'; (3) the seducing from their allegiance of the armed forces of the Crown.
>
> "The ultimate object of the doctrine of Communism is the overthrow of capitalism and the establishment of the dictatorship of the proletariat."

He added in all seriousness that one of the accused had been heard to say that he hoped to see the Red Flag flying over Buckingham Palace.

This long jumble of political illiteracy was not addressed to the jury, for there was of course no jury in that Court. It was both unnecessary and inappropriate as an address to the magistrate, who was a trained lawyer whose only duty was to hear the evidence and determine whether it disclosed a *prima facie* case for trial by a jury. It was obviously a political speech, probably drafted in its main lines in the Home Office, and designed to make the public flesh creep and to frighten all actual or potential members or supporters of the Communist Party. One must not blame the prosecuting counsel for it, for he no doubt believed it and was happy to say it; he later became a High Court judge, known for extremely reactionary views, and was in fact the judge who tried the case of the South Wales Communists which I describe later in this chapter.

The accused were released on bail during the police Court proceedings and while awaiting trial at the Central Criminal Court—something which perhaps would not happen now, when everything in the class war has become cruder. It was on this occasion that George Bernard Shaw, who was one of the sureties, answered the usual question from the Clerk: "Are you worth £100?" with his now famous remark: "Well, I have that much money."

At the Central Criminal Court, the charges against the accused were formulated in the Indictment in three Counts, as follows:

1. conspiracy to publish and utter seditious libels and words;

2. conspiring to incite persons to commit breaches of the Incitement to Mutiny Act, 1797;

3. conspiring to endeavour to seduce from their duty persons serving in His Majesty's forces to whom might come certain publications, to wit the *Workers' Weekly*" (the forerunner of the *Daily Worker*) "and others, and to incite them to mutiny."

The prosecuting counsel at the trial was the then Attorney-General, Sir Douglas Hogg, afterwards Lord Chancellor.*

* His political attitude can be shown by the fact that when, in a casual conversation with me, with whom he had up to then been on reasonably friendly terms, he learnt that I was at that time a member of the Labour Party, he was so profoundly shocked that he raised his hand to slap my face, and only just pulled himself up in time.

His speech was much on the lines of that made in the police Court.

The judge was notoriously a bitter reactionary, and had been a Tory member of Parliament. All the accused were convicted, and he made to some of them, openly from the Bench, an offer not to send them to prison if they would renounce Communism! Naturally, none of them accepted the offer, and the judge then sentenced them all to terms of imprisonment long enough to keep them out of public activity over the period when the general strike was expected to—and did—take place.

In fulfilment of my promise to illustrate the reluctance of the ruling class to prosecute its own members for treason, I now come to an illustration which proves to be strangely linked with this prosecution of the twelve Communists. It involves going back to the weeks before the outbreak of the First World War, at a time when proposals were from time to time put forward by Liberal governments to grant Ireland a measure of self-government, labelled "Home Rule". This modest proposal to give some small concession to England's oldest and very cruelly mishandled colony excited vehement opposition from the Tories, and even from a section of the Liberal Party, which in the end broke away, labelled itself "Liberal Unionist", and gradually merged in the Tory Party (the word "Unionist", which is often used of the Tory Party, stems from this). Vehement opposition also came in Ireland itself from the Protestant section of the population of Ulster, which had originally been planted there by Cromwell, on "divide and rule" principles, to help in holding down the rest of Ireland.

Shortly before the First World War began in 1914, the then Liberal government, led by H. H. Asquith and including Lloyd George and Winston Churchill, was firmly proposing to carry through Parliament a "Home Rule" Bill, and the angry Conservatives and other reactionaries started to prepare various forms of illegal resistance. The first was a conspiracy of English army officers, at a large military base in Southern Ireland called "The Curragh" where some of the English troops thought necessary to hold down the population were stationed, to refuse to obey orders or to march against Ulster in the event —then very likely—that Protestant elements in Ulster would break out in treasonable rebellion if the Home Rule Bill became law. These officers should have been court martialled for conspiracy to commit breaches of the Incitement to Mutiny Act, 1797, and for other offences; but they were "gentlemen", and it was unthinkable—to the ruling class—that they should be prosecuted as criminals. The Home Secretary of the day pusillanimously negotiated with them and agreed not to prosecute them (his name was Winston Churchill).

The next criminal preparation for resistance was a conspiracy, forming as we shall see a neat contrast to the prosecution just related of the twelve Communists, which was if possible even more blatantly treasonable than that of the "gentlemen" at "The Curragh". It was led by a group of "gentlemen" (of whom incidentally only one was Irish, and he was not an Ulsterman). Their activities included large scale gun-running into Ulster and the open organisation and training of an "Ulster Volunteer Force", designed to "levy war against the King in his realm", as the law of treason describes it. Part of the treasonable activity was the delivery of inflammatory speeches, some of which I must quote. The first came as early as the 22nd January, 1912, in Liverpool, a town outside Ireland, but having a large Irish population. One F. E. Smith, afterwards Lord Chancellor Birkenhead, who was not Irish but a Merseyside Englishman, then said:

"There is no length to which Ulster will not be entitled to go —however desperate or unconstitutional—if the quarrel is wickedly fixed upon them—" (i.e., if the Parliament of Great Britain and Ireland, in which Ulster as well as the rest of Ireland was represented, passed the proposed legislation) —"and I say without hesitation that in any resistance to which Ulster might be driven, rather than submit to Home Rule on which the constituencies have not been consulted, she would command your support and she would command my support, and I am the last man in the world to recommend any other man to take risks which I would not be prepared myself to share."

He was not prosecuted. He must have known that he would not be, for he was enrolled among the "gentlemen" of the ruling class.

The next noteworthy speech came in Oxfordshire on the

27th July, 1912, from Sir Edward Carson, of Irish origin, who had emigrated from Dublin to London to seek and find fame as a barrister. He said:

> "We will shortly challenge the Government to interfere with us if they dare, and we will with equanimity await the result. We will do this regardless of all consequences, of all personal loss, or of all inconveniences. They may tell us, if they like, that that is treason. It is not for such men, who have such issues at stake as we have, to trouble about the cost. We are prepared to take the consequences, and in the struggle we will not be alone, because we have the best in England with us."

Brave words? Brave treasonable words? Well, we must measure the bravery by our knowledge, and still more by Carson's knowledge, of the remoteness of the risk of his being arrested and prosecuted.

Soon after, at Lisburn, County Antrim, in Ulster itself, Sir Edward Carson made another speech, on the 19th September, 1912:

> "I promise you, with all the sacred confidence that you and I ought to feel towards one another, that if this (Home Rule) policy is persisted in there is no length that may be necessary, no sacrifice that may be compulsory, that I and others who are associated with me are not prepared to take in the defence of Ireland."

The "defence of Ireland", if you please, was the criminal resistance to the proposal that Ireland should be put in the position of governing herself.

Of course, he was not prosecuted, and he went on to say in Coleraine two days later:

> "Here is what the Covenant says: 'In the event of such a Bill being forced upon us we further solemnly and mutually pledge ourselves not to recognise its authority.' I do not care twopence whether it is treason or not; it is what we are going to do."

He did not care twopence, for he felt safe; and a few months later, on the 16th May, 1913, in the inflammable city of Belfast, he said:

> "Go, be ready. You are our great army. It is on you we rely. You must trust us to select the most opportune methods for, if necessary, taking over the whole government of the community in which we live. I know a great deal of that will involve statutory liability, but it will also involve moral righteousness."

Further and further he went, without prosecution, and without fear of it. On the 7th September, 1913, he told another meeting:

> "I do not hesitate to tell you that you ought to set yourselves against the constituted authority in the land. . . . But the danger and the difficulties will be great. There will be the danger and the difficulties of trying to run a government of our own against the constituted authority under the Home Rule Bill. . . . We will set up that government—I am told it will be illegal. Of course it will. Drilling is illegal; I was reading an Act of Parliament forbidding it.* The Volunteers are illegal, and the Government know they are illegal, and the Government dare not interfere with them. . . .
>
> "Don't be afraid of illegalities; illegalities are not crimes when they are taken to assert what is the elementary right of every citizen, the protection of his freedom,† and if anyone tells me I should be ashamed of myself, I tell him it is the motive I live for, and if I am threatened I am prepared to defend myself. . . . We will not allow any individual or any body of men, whether they call themselves a Parliament or a Government, to take away what we consider essential for the carrying on of our rights and privileges."

F. E. Smith, who had meanwhile been appointed as a "galloper" in the Ulster Volunteer Force, which Carson had

---

* The Unlawful Drilling Act, 1819, mentioned above, rendered him liable *if* he were prosecuted and convicted, to seven years in prison.

† I have heard a good many definitions of freedom. As used here it means in effect the right to refuse to let your fellow-Irishmen have and exercise the right to govern themselves rather than to remain a colony of England.

described as "illegal", and was in fact a treasonable and organised armed force intended to resist the lawful government of the country, was in County Antrim at about the same time as Carson, and on the 20th September, 1913, he said in one of his speeches there:

"Home Rule will be dead for ever on the day when 100,000 men" he meant the Ulster Volunteer Force—"armed with rifles assemble at Balmoral (Belfast)."

In another speech on the same day, he said:

"From that moment" (the passing of the Home Rule Act), "we on our part will say to our followers in England: 'To your tents, O Israel!' From that moment we shall stand side by side with you, refusing to recognise any law, and prepared with you to risk the collapse of the whole body politic to prevent this monstrous crime. The sands are running down in the glass. The time has arrived for action on your part and ours."

A fortnight later, in Armagh, on the 4th October, 1913, Smith repeated:

"We shall make England realise that" (the establishment of a Home Rule Parliament) "can never be done, the more easily, the more swiftly, and the more triumphantly your Volunteer movement advances. I hope to see at an early date those men who have undergone the necessary discipline and drill armed with real rifles. On the day on which there will be in Ulster 100,000 disciplined men armed with rifles, wherever else Home Rule may be talked about, it will never be talked of in Ulster."

Sir William Joynson-Hicks, mentioned above, did not want to be left behind. At Warrington, in Lancashire, on the 6th December, 1913, he thus allied the Tory Party, God and plain treason:

"The people of Ulster have behind them the Unionist Party. Behind them is the Lord God of Battles. In his name and your name I say to the Prime Minister: 'Let your armies and batteries fire. Fire if you dare; fire and be damned!' "*

I come back to Sir Edward Carson. On the 17th January, 1914, at a review in Belfast of the "East Belfast Regiment" of the treasonable Ulster Volunteer Force (think for a moment how far the Communist Party, or the T.U.C., would be allowed to get in efforts to hold a review of their armed rebels, if they wanted any) he exhorted the "troops" thus:

"I want you all to reflect that day by day and hour by hour we are coming nearer the great crisis for which we have been so long preparing" (he was not referring to the First World War, which any serious politician could see approaching, but to the proposal to give a measure of self-government to Ireland), "and I notice that the nearer we approach that day the more your courage and my courage and your determination and mine grows; I tell them (the Government) that if they dare to come and attack us red blood will flow."

Not long afterwards, the First World War broke out, in which the wealth and power of capitalist Britain and its ruling class were at stake, the Home Rule Bill was dropped, and to outward seeming the Ulster movement faded away. But there remained the fact, or the alleged fact that, at a time when the British army which had to fight in Europe was dreadfully short of rifles there were in Ulster something like 100,000 modern rifles available. (I had myself always doubted whether there were many of these rifles in existence at all, and whether what there were were second-hand stuff of the sort that so often turned up in gun-running experience; but when I was in Ulster some forty years later a "respectable" Ulsterman who had no reason to mislead me told me that they really existed, that they were the most modern rifles available—supplied from Germany—and that he had had many of them stored in his own cellar.)

* In 1925, when a vote of censure was moved on the then government for having launched the prosecution of the twelve Communists described above, Joynson-Hicks was firmly reminded of this speech. He was good enough to say that he regretted having made the speech, and added: "I at all events was not involved in any of the activities", i.e., he was prepared to incite treason, but not actually to take part. How noble! Perhaps it was fitting that he was later ennobled by being sent to the House of Lords.

It was widely believed at the time that Carson's patriotism, switched to the European circuit now that his Ulster problem was no longer urgent, had led him to hand the rifles to the British government; but he would not allow this story to be accepted. On the 28th September, 1914, he said in a speech:

> "When the war is over we will call our Provisional Government together and we will repeal the Home Rule Bill as far as it concerns us in ten minutes. All our Ulster Volunteers are going to kick out anybody who tries to put it into force in Ulster. . . . We also have with us our guns. I heard somebody say we had allowed the guns to go out of Ulster. It is a lie. Not a single gun has gone out of Ulster, nor a single round of ammunition. So long as I am leader I will consent to bringing in any amount of guns, but I will never consent to a single gun leaving Ulster."

And, to make it clear that the Tory Party in general stood firm in treason no matter what might happen to the larger war, Mr. Bonar Law, another Tory leader who was not an Irishman, said at the same meeting:

> "We (i.e., the Unionist Party) shall support you to the last in any steps which Sir Edward Carson and your leaders think it is necessary for you to take to defend your rights. . . . We give the pledge without any conditions."

The link with the prosecution of the twelve Communists, and the contrast of which I wrote between the enforcement of "law" against their opponents in the class war and the indulgence displayed by the ruling class towards blatant treason from their own members is shown by the following facts:

Of the government which prosecuted the twelve Communists, the treasonable "Galloper Smith" was Lord Chancellor, the treasonable Joynson-Hicks was Home Secretary, and the treasonable Bonar Law would have been a member had he lived long enough, and the treasonable Carson would have been a member had he not meanwhile been appointed a Lord of Appeal, i.e., a judge in the House of Lords.

The next case I have to relate (the one in which W. H. Thompson had given me the warning about the atmosphere of political cases which I described in Chapter 2, above) was a charge against a group of Communists from South Wales of various offences in the nature of "incitement to mutiny". It illustrates mainly how prosecuting authorities behave in the preparation of cases, and also the attitude of some judges.

The malpractice started even before the Indictment was drawn. The case ought to have been tried in Monmouthshire, for it is a very old and good rule of criminal procedure that cases should be tried in the county where they arise. But some of the accused were well-known and even popular in that area, and might well have been acquitted by a local jury; so the government, bent on securing convictions, applied to the Court for an order, which was granted, to transfer the case to the Central Criminal Court in London, where the accused were unknown. It gave as its ground that it might be difficult to get a fair trial in Monmouthshire (which caused a wry smile among those who thought that the last thing a government wants in a political case is a fair trial).

The next bit of malpractice was that a copy of the Indictment, the document which tells the accused, and tells each of them, exactly what charge is made against them, was not delivered until 4.30 p.m. on the day before the trial. Such copies are normally delivered, in a case of any substance, some days before the hearing. Normally they are not very important because they do no more than put into specific legal form the charges on which the magistrates have committed the accused for trial, but it is always necessary to have a copy in good time, lest the offences charged in the Indictment should prove to be enlarged or altered since the committal. W. H. Thompson, never failing a client and never trusting a government, had been pressing for a copy day by day for a week, being put off all the time with excuses: "Sorry, it's not quite ready; perhaps tomorrow."

When the copy finally arrived, it turned out that the most important of the accused, who had decided to conduct his own defence whilst I represented the others, had been quietly promoted in the Indictment from a charge of a minor offence, punishable with a maximum of one year's imprisonment, to one of a major offence punishable with life imprisonment. Such a change, if the prosecution relies only on the evidence given before the magistrates, with perhaps minor additional witnesses of whose evidence adequate and precise advance notice must be given, is admissible in law, but it would never have been made at such short notice in a non-political case. In this case, it raised problems for the defence. Now that this important accused had been raised into a high danger zone, should he continue to defend himself, or should I now defend him along with the rest, or should he be separately represented by another barrister, who would need to study the case? Thompson and I concluded that we must get the case adjourned for a few days, in order to decide this question and if necessary get new counsel to study the man's case. Thompson doubted whether the judge would give an adjournment; I said that he could not refuse, as the whole trouble was caused by the misbehaviour of the prosecution, and he replied: "You wait and see!" The next morning the judge, a man of great experience and knowledge of the criminal law, so bitterly opposed to anything left-wing that he would have had great difficulty in giving a fair trial if he had wanted to do so, listened impatiently and with a good deal of interruption to my request for an adjournment and to my statement of the grounds for it. He even said that the alteration of the charge made no difference. I retorted that until the prosecution acted on that view by dropping the new charge, I should continue to regard the difference as one between a one-year maximum and possible life imprisonment. We went on for some time, and at one stage he said: "Do you realise that, if I were to grant you this adjournment, at least one day of judicial time would be wasted?" I replied that no doubt he would rebuke the prosecution for causing this waste, but that he might consider the waste of a day's judicial time a lesser evil than a day spent in causing injustice to accused persons who had not had the time to prepare to meet the new situation.

The judge remained adamant, so I played my last card. Every accused has the right to "challenge" anyone summoned to sit on a jury, i.e., to refuse to have that person on the jury; and some of these challenges are called "peremptory", which means that the challenge is valid without any reason having to be given for it. The Court officials summon a fair number of jurors over and above the actual requirements, in case there may be challenges, but wholesale challenges are rare, and they certainly do not summon enough jurors to cover them. If the judge did not give way I could still get a day's adjournment by letting the jurors be called up into the jury box one by one— the right moment for "challenge"—and challenging the first sixty, namely twelve for each of the five accused. There were probably not sixty jurors still waiting at this stage of the morning, if there ever had been; and it would have needed twelve more than that to constitute a jury to try the case.

I could not threaten the judge directly that I would do this, so I "stage-whispered" to my junior that I would. The judge, not wanting this public advertisement of his behaviour, simply said in an icy voice: "I will grant an adjournment until to-morrow morning." This gave us time, and we decided that I would now defend all the accused, instead of all but one, and the case went on to the inevitable convictions and sentences, with no particular departure from normal behaviour on the part of the judge or the prosecution, except for one bit of "window-dressing" by the latter. One of the witnesses who was alleged to have been given a copy of an offending class-war pamphlet was a "territorial" soldier, that is, a civilian who served in camp, in uniform, for one week a year, and for the rest went on with his civilian job and drilled occasionally in the evenings. This man went into the witness-box not in his normal civilian clothes, but in full uniform with buttons beautifully polished and accoutrements "blancoed", looking the picture of an innocent soldier to whom someone has basely tried to talk peace. When I asked him why he had come in uniform, he replied that he had been ordered to do so.

I now travel as far as what is now Pakistan, to a Royal Air Force court martial case illustrating a number of malpractices, which could have occurred in criminal proceedings in England, and still more in colonial proceedings. It was by no means the only scandal that emerged in the immediate post-Second World War period in connection with courts martial, but I feel that it had a greater variety of faults than any other that has come to my notice.

The principal but not the only victim in this case was one Leading Aircraftsman Attwood, who was accused of incitement to mutiny in respect of certain events which occurred at the large R.A.F. station at Drigh Road, Karachi (then in British

India). I and other lawyers and M.Ps., and Attwood's trade union, the Electrical Trades Union, in the end achieved a great deal, both directly for Attwood and other men accused at the same time, and generally. Our efforts indeed led to the establishment of the Courts Martial Appeal Tribunal, mentioned in Chapter 7 of Book 2.

I begin with the events which led up to the court martial of Attwood. Dissatisfaction was rife at that time among the men at Drigh Road, mainly owing to delays in demobilisation, although there were also complaints of excessive overtime working, of "spit and polish", and of very bad food. The first collective manifestation of grievances came on the 17th January, 1946, when a general meeting of the men on the station was held after dusk; about 900 were present. Attwood, a level-headed man of common sense, and an active trade unionist in peacetime, had nothing to do with the calling of the meeting, but he attended it, and was one of two dozen or so speakers. There was talk of a strike; Attwood opposed this suggestion, but supported the proposal that the dissatisfaction should be expressed by parading on the following Saturday, the 19th January, in khaki drill uniform instead of in "best blue".

The idea of striking was dropped, and the parade suggestion was carried out. As a result, the Commanding Officer listened to the complaints, which were voiced on behalf of all the men by a number of them, including Attwood, and agreed to get the Air Officer Commanding to visit the station as soon as possible to consider them. There was, in fact, on the evening of that Saturday, a further meeting of some of the men; it was a smaller meeting, and was said to have decided on strike action. Attwood was not present.

It was soon learnt that the Air Officer Commanding was to visit the station on Monday the 21st January, and another meeting was held on the evening before, attended by 1,000 men. At that meeting all idea of striking was definitely abandoned, and the points to be put to the A.O.C. on the following day were formulated. Attwood spoke at this meeting, strongly and successfully opposing the idea of striking.

On the Monday, the A.O.C. duly arrived, and received a delegation of the men; he promised expressly that there should be no victimisation. As will be seen later, this promise was of the greatest importance. After two and a half hours of discussion, the A.O.C., repeating the pledge of no victimisation, agreed to take up the grievances about demobilisation and to allow a petition to the Prime Minister, Mr. Attlee, to be organised and sent; and he dealt reasonably with other matters, too.

The petition was signed by 1,205 men in the course of that week, and sent off. The food improved at once, and other matters were remedied; and there was no more talk of a strike. Not a minute of working-time had been lost, and the men's complaints had been sincerely met.

On the following Saturday, the 26th January, 1946, the C.O. of the station addressed the men, emphasising the seriousness of what had taken place; he assured them once again that there would be no victimisation.

One might not have expected that the upper ranks of the commanding officers, with long years of service and old-fashioned idea of discipline, would think of any more subtle remedies for grievances than kit-inspections, parades, drills, discipline, and "spit and polish". But the conduct of some of these officers when confronted with rumours of strikes proved to be more understanding than might have been feared; probably they grasped the genuineness and depth of the grievances and did not want the situation to get out of hand. Certainly, up to that Saturday, the authorities, i.e., the C.O. of the station, the A.O.C., and all other high officers who were concerned with the trouble, behaved with honesty, foresight and intelligence. What was soon to come was far distant from any of those virtues.

Sinister things began to happen. Somewhere high up, somebody—a forerunner of Senator McCarthy, a Colonel Blimp, or just an idiot—perhaps alarmed by the strikes and threats of strikes that were cropping up in many Army and Air Force stations in many areas, set to work with a complete lack of human understanding and fair-dealing. Within a week of that 26th January a Court of Enquiry was held at Drigh Road, at which a number of officers were questioned, together with Attwood and one other aircraftsman whom I will call M. The questions put to these two were formal and unobjectionable, and everyone still thought that the matter was at an end. As it turned out, this was a sad mistake. Some two months later, by which time the C.O. who had behaved so reasonably had been replaced, a number of members of the Special Intelligence Branch (S.I.B.) of the Air Force, who had probably been on the station for some time under camouflage, came into the open and began to interview large numbers of men.

I was receiving at that time, in my capacity as an M.P., a good many complaints from various stations of the activities of the S.I.B., which was in effect a body of police investigators. At home, there are many good checks on such bodies; they can be criticised by defending solicitors and counsel, by judges, and by the National Council for Civil Liberties; and the press can often come in too. They can be challenged quickly by parliamentary questions. When they give evidence, they do so in public, before magistrates or judges, and in the presence of the press. And convictions based on their evidence have to be reached by regular Courts, and are subject to judicial appeals. If their conduct even in those conditions frequently leads to complaints, it is easy to imagine how some of them behaved 5,000 miles away, virtually free of all these checks, when dealing with servicemen who could not easily get independent legal advice, could be hampered in their efforts to communicate with their families, their friends, their trade unions, or Members of Parliament, and would be tried by courts martial, generally staffed by officers without legal experience, sitting only theoretically in public and arriving at convictions which at that time could be challenged only by written petitions and not by any form of judicial appeal. It is not surprising that these investigators, at Drigh Road and elsewhere, acted on the assumption that their superiors were interested in results and were not squeamish about the methods used to get them.

The investigators' general line was to tell the men that they would prevent them getting home unless they "came clean", without of course telling them that if they did "come clean" the S.I.B. would do all it could to secure that they did not get home—except as convicts—for many years. They even told men who had merely attended one of the meetings that they were liable to long terms of imprisonment, and would certainly serve such terms if they did not give further information. They made such remarks as "It probably won't be the death-penalty now that the war is over", and referred to men in other stations

E

who, they said, "had nearly been shot". They asked the men
how their wives would get on without separation allowances
whilst they were in prison; and they put one man who refused
to sign a statement into the Guard Room and kept him there
until he agreed to do so. They suggested that the "men who led
the demonstration" (i.e., those who had put forward the
proposal to parade in khaki drill and had been promised
that there would be no victimisation) would be "on the other
side in the next war". Most of the men being interrogated by
such methods were young and inexperienced, did not know the
powers of the S.I.B., and did not know—and were of course not
told—that they were entitled to refuse to answer questions, and
to seek legal advice. Attwood himself, an intelligent man with
the confidence born of his knowledge that he had a good militant trade union to back him, told the investigators that he
would not make any statement as he had, in common with the
rest, had a promise of no victimisation.

At home, the methods used would be sure to lead to the
statements being excluded by the Court, or to any convictions
based on them being upset on appeal; but the S.I.B. were not
foolish in hoping that out in India they might get away with
it. We shall see how nearly they did so.

Attwood and a number of other airmen at Drigh Road, all
of whom had been promised that there would be no victimisation, were questioned by the S.I.B. men. They were all due for
early repatriation and demobilisation, were deeply interested
in that, and not much in anything else. They were thus
peculiarly vulnerable to the investigators' suggestions that their
return home would be delayed indefinitely if they did not say,
and say quickly, what the investigators wanted to hear.

Attwood himself had got as far, by the 10th March, 1946,
shortly before the S.I.B. came into the open, as to sign the first
stage of his release papers at Drigh Road. About the end of
March, after his questioning by the S.I.B. was finished, he was
actually sent to the transit camp at Worli, near Bombay,
whence men flew or sailed to Britain. I had meanwhile received
many reports of the conduct of the S.I.B. men, and had raised
the matter in the House of Commons, finding the ministers on
the defensive and obviously uneasy. By the 10th April, 1946,
Attwood had been arrested and charged with "incitement to

mutiny", and placed in solitary confinement in a detention camp at Kalyan, near Bombay but some 800 miles from Drigh Road, where his lawyers, when he could get some, would have to search for witnesses for his defence. There follows a long and complicated story of the efforts of Attwood himself, his friends in England, including myself, and his comrades at Drigh Road and his union here, to see that he was properly defended, which involved getting money, finding good—and they proved to be very good—Indian lawyers in Bombay, and overcoming the difficulties created by what one can only call the deliberate and systematic sabotage by the Air Force authorities of his attempts (and those of his friends) to communicate with one another through the post. I must pass over these, and come to the actual course of his trial, which was interesting and sinister enough. When Attwood, after all the many troubles and obstacles, actually appeared before the court martial, the lawyers from Bombay, who had had very little time to prepare, relied on the defence of "condonation", which meant in effect that the promises of no victimisation which I have described above barred the prosecution. They convinced the Court that this defence was sound, and on the 14th May, 1946, it was accepted by the Court, Attwood was released, and the decision was referred to the Air Officer Commanding, Bangalore, for confirmation, the Court adjourning meanwhile. This was the normal procedure, since confirmation is necessary. But it was assumed to be merely a formality, as the decision was one of fact, arrived at by a Court which had heard the witnesses, the evidence was clear, and there seemed to be no ground for not affirming the acquittal.

One might have thought that by now the trouble was over, but "Blimp" had his way, and the "confirming authority" at Bangalore did not confirm the acquittal. It directed that Attwood should be re-arrested, and the court martial reconvened to try him for the alleged incitement to mutiny.

When the re-trial began, the President of the Court, who, as was established, had had a personal conversation with the "confirming authority" at Bangalore before the further proceedings began, displayed considerable hostility to the defending lawyers (who made a very spirited protest), and—quite illegally—ordered the representatives of Reuters and the press

generally not to report the protest. After this, the Court heard
the evidence, which came out strongly in Attwood's favour, for
as we have seen he had really in effect been earnestly inciting
his comrades *not* to strike. Nevertheless, the Court maintained
its hostility, and found him guilty.

This seemed like the blackest moment in a long tale of injustice; but of course this decision, like the other, required
confirmation by the "confirming authority", and this confirmation never came. Soon afterwards, Attwood was told that he
was free, and could return to England. Confirming authorities
do not give reasons for their decisions, and we shall never know
what led them into the paths of justice in this unexpected
fashion. It may have been the strength of the evidence, or
public indignation at home, or pressure from M.P.s or the
trade union, or a combination of all these factors. It is significant
that two other men, involved in somewhat similar incidents in
Kanpur, and awaiting trial at the same time as Attwood, were
told at this time that proceedings against them were being
dropped.

The next court martial case I have to relate was that at Tel-
el-Kebir in Egypt, some months later in the year 1946, and
fairly classified as a "demobilisation strike". It arose out of the
sudden announcement on the 7th November, 1946, of further
delays in demobilisation, at Tel-el-Kebir, a large ordnance base
in Egypt, on the road from Cairo to Ismailia; on this occasion
I acted as defence counsel. After some anxieties, it ended in the
acquittal of all the men involved.

The camp in question was a large permanent one, containing
some 3,000 British troops, mostly R.A.O.C. and R.E.M.E.
(i.e., ordnance and engineering workers), engaged largely on
industrial work. There were also a number of German prisoners
of war,* doing much of the domestic work of the camp, and
many thousands of Egyptian civilians from the neighbouring
villages, coming in to work by the day.

From Thursday 7th to Monday 11th November, inclusive,
there was unrest among the British troops in the camp as a
result of the announcement of delays in demobilisation; it was
manifested solely by the abstention by the bulk of the British

* "God save the King" was played in the Officers' Mess every evening by
German prisoners.

troops from their industrial work. According to no less than ten prosecution witnesses, including Lt.-Col. Strong, the C.O. of the camp, the vitally necessary duty of explaining to the men, who in peacetime were industrial workers to whom a strike is a lawful and normal part of life, the illegality of strikes in the Army, the meaning of "mutiny", and the provisions of the Army Act generally, had been wholly neglected, and none of them knew about these matters. In the eye of military law, their strike no doubt amounted to mutiny; to them, it was devoid of any criminality. What looked like a conspiracy to keep them in this dangerous ignorance was probably only incompetence or neglect of duty on the part of a number of officers.

During the five days in question, there was no disorder, no violence, no insult to or assault on any officer or N.C.O., no injury to property, not even a tea-cup or a pane of glass broken, and no failure to fulfil any military duty of any kind (if a distinction can fairly be drawn between military and industrial duties, as the C.O. said in evidence that it could), and no person other than British troops was ever directly or indirectly involved. (It was never suggested in any way by the prosecution that the accused or any of them ever conspired or intended to cause any disorder, nor even that disorder was likely to result from what they were alleged to have done.)

The strike came to a peaceful end, and "investigations" of the familiar type then began, the principal investigator this time being one Major H. Some eighty-nine men were questioned in all, including the ten men who were ultimately prosecuted. Statements were obtained from them by methods not very different from those employed at Drigh Road, with the added and especial horror that many of them were "persuaded" to make statements by being confined in the abandoned punishment cells of a German prisoner-of-war camp at a place called Tahag. There was plenty of room for them in various guard rooms in Tel-el-Kebir itself, and some of the men were kept there; plenty too in other camps near by, and some were kept there; plenty also in relatively habitable hutments at Tahag itself. But some dozens were put in these punishment cells. The cells were cement boxes, some of them 5 ft. by 10 ft. others 6 ft. by 8 ft. Their only light and ventilation came through slits

4 in. by 2 in., high up in the walls, 10 ft. or more from the ground, and through the "Judas" holes in the doors. They were in an indescribable state of filth. The men were kept in these cells, sometimes two to a cell although other cells were empty, for 23 hours out of the 24, with no lights, nothing to read, and nothing to do. The smell was appalling. They were taken out of the cells at intervals and asked if they would make statements; some who made statements were removed to better quarters, and those who did not do so were told: "You are mugs to stay in here whilst others are outside", and one high officer who called daily to ask about statements, was heard to say: "Coo, what a blue-pencil smell! No wonder you lads are making statements." Under these "inducements", a good many men made statements, and most of those who did so were released. Some of them afterwards appeared as witnesses at the court martial, and some as accused.

When the business of "investigation" was over, ten men were selected to be charged. Up to that point, the story was in the main one of cruelty and brutality; as it developed thereafter, it presented a picture—I am sorry to say not unusual—of stupidity and injustice. As for the taking of statements, the principal defect, apart from the Tahag "treament" itself, was that of improper pressure on the lines we have seen already at Drigh Road, and in, my view, which was confirmed by the ultimate acquittal of all the men charged, all the statements used at the trial were inadmissible. As the cross-examination of the prosecution witnesses went on, it became clearer and clearer that the improper conduct of Major H. was an important feature of the case, and I asked where he was. I was told that he had been allowed to return to England. I snorted loudly when I heard this hoary old trick, and finally the prosecution decided to fetch him back from England to give evidence. A day or two later, it told the Court that he had actually arrived in Egypt, but could not reach the Court on the following day, and they asked for an adjournment of one day (as their other evidence was all finished). This was granted, but when we reassembled after the adjournment Major H. was not there, the prosecution gave no explanation, and did not ask for any further adjournment. He was never called, and we never learnt what had happened to him or to the proposal to call him. One could only assume that some person of intelligence had examined him and concluded that what he would have to admit if he went into the witness-box would have an even worse effect on the prosecution case than the bad one created by the failure to produce him!*

How the particular ten men were chosen for prosecution was a mystery. There was neither less nor more evidence against them than there would have been against any other group picked at random, for all the R.A.O.C. and R.E.M.E. men had taken part in the strike, and there was nothing to show that any of the ten chosen had done any more than that. They were all young industrial workers, only one of them being over 22. They came from all ranges of politics and many parts of Britain. Most of them had been in the cells at Tahag, and all of them had a very clear idea of the horrors of military prisons. But their morale and their brains were very good, and I found it a pleasure to work with them.

The charge was an extraordinary concoction, but I never discovered any more sinister reason for its curious framing than stupidity. The general picture of the strike being—as it came out in the evidence—that for five days the men quietly abstained from doing any industrial work, the charges against the ten accused were not directly charges of mutiny, nor with any offence at all covering the first two days of the strike, but were charges of "conspiring with other persons to cause a mutiny . . . in that they at Tel-el-Kebir Garrison, on or about 9th and 10th November" (i.e., on the third and fourth days of the strike) "conspired together and with other soldiers unknown to cause a mutiny . . . that is to say, the resistance of lawful military authority by refusing to carry out their lawful duties on 11th November" (i.e., on the fifth and last day!).

There was no evidence of any of the "conspirators" holding secret meetings, or any such activity, either on the 9th and 10th or at any other time. It may be suspected, with a strike so well organised and so tidily and peacefully carried through, that

* When I was flying back to England ten days later, a man in the uniform of a major approached me, and told me that he was H., that it was a thousand pities he had not been called, and that if he had been he would quickly have shown that his behaviour had been proper, and all my clients would have been convicted. This was too much for me, and I replied that if I had had the pleasure of cross-examining him for half an hour he would have had a "bowler hat" within a week. (A bowler hat is Army slang for dismissal from the service.)

there were some persons of rank and age managing things in the background, and that the "high-ups" were anxious that no officers should be exposed as being the originators of the trouble. This might explain a lot of gaps, but it would still not explain the curious framing of the charge.

After the evidence had failed to prove anything of great importance, the Court acquitted four of the accused, and convicted the other six. Once again, it was not easy to see how the four were selected.

I told the six convicted men that I would get their convictions quashed, and that they would be released. I was right, and I think that they believed me, but their faces showed that the prospect of even a few weeks in a military prison was terrifying. When I got back to England, I immediately prepared the necessary Petition, and within the relatively short period of two months the convictions were all quashed on the ground that the statements extracted from the men were inadmissible in evidence.

The misbehaviour of the military authorities was not yet exhausted. Scarcely a letter I wrote to the men, even those containing copies of the Petition, was delivered, and almost every letter they sent to me suffered the same fate. And, when the President of the court martial had the duty to inform the men in open Court that the convictions had been quashed and that they were free men, he began by informing them of the sentences that had been passed on them; and only then—after they had had time to take in this awful news—did he tell them that "the convictions had not been confirmed". And the men's pay, which had been stopped pending their trial, was held up for some time before it reached them. But, after all, they won.

I return to England, and go back in time to 1934, to deal with the next cases I have to relate, those of Tom Mann and Harry Pollitt at the Glamorgan Assizes. The misbehaviour in these cases was confined to the work of those who decided to launch the prosecutions; the actual conduct of the trial at Swansea was without fault.

The background of the prosecutions was the prolonged unemployment and slump of the 'thirties. The National Unemployed Workers' Movement, had been founded—when it was seen that mass unemployment for long and indefinite periods was likely to be a standing feature of our capitalist "way of life", now called "the free world"—in order to represent the special interests of the unemployed, and to help in maintaining their morale under circumstances which would break that of almost anyone. In 1934, it organised a number of Hunger Marches of thousands of unemployed from all over Britain to London, to meet there in a mighty demonstration in Hyde Park on the 25th February, designed to compel the government to take measures to reduce unemployment and in other ways to relieve their terrible situation (it has been forgotten by many of us that the unemployment pay for an adult male at that time was 15s. 3d. per week). Governments are always alarmed by great demonstrations, and this government was eager to stop this one being held. It had no power to forbid it, and any attempt to take such power by Act of Parliament, or even to use the police on some pretext to prevent the marchers assembling, would have produced tremendous hostility. So, as always, it sought to achieve its object by indirect means; it tried to "dispose of" Pollitt and Mann, who were to receive the marchers in London and to address the demonstration. They were both well-loved working-class leaders and magnificent speakers. Pollitt was the general secretary of the Communist Party, and Mann was, among other things, treasurer of the National Unemployed Workers' Movement. If the government could somehow ensure their absence from the demonstration, it would have achieved something, from its point of view. The two men were in fact on a tour of South Wales, addressing public meetings with their usual forthrightness, and in particular they both made speeches on Sunday the 18th February, just a week before the date fixed for the demonstration in Hyde Park, and six days before Pollitt was to address an important "Congress of Action", also in London. So the government, having of course had reports from the police of the speeches they had both made on the 18th, swooped on them as late as the 23rd, the day before the "Congress of Action" meeting was to be addressed by Pollitt. The police arrested them both at their homes in or near London, took them down to Glamorganshire, and charged them on the Saturday before the magistrates with sedition, alleged to have been committed in their speeches on the previous Sunday. I have already fully described the law of sedition, with all its uncertainties and difficulties, in Chapter 1, above; and I think it fair to say that no prosecuting authority with anything more to gain by a prosecution than the possibility of a conviction would have dreamt of prosecuting anyone for saying what Pollitt and Mann had said. But here the Government had the possibility of hampering the Hunger Marches and of half-muzzling the two leaders, not just for a few days but for the weeks which would elapse before the case could come on at the Assizes.

On that Saturday, the magistrates remanded the two men for a week. They could hardly dare to refuse bail, but they fixed it rather high, and gave a broad hint that further bail after the adjourned hearing would depend on the activities, or inactivity, of the accused in the meantime. It was by then too late for Pollitt to address the Congress of Action, and it was thought wiser that neither he nor Mann should address the demonstration; so the government had already made one or two illegitimate gains. But it made no more, and it now faced the awkward situation that it had to go forward with prosecutions on very weak evidence, with nothing to comfort it but the knowledge that middle-class or lower middle-class juries are prone to convict Communists even on very weak evidence. (I discussed juries in detail in Chapter 9 of Book 2.)

It was decided that, as Mann's case stood above Pollitt's in the Assize List, and must therefore be tried first, I should defend Mann, and not Pollitt. If I got Mann off, the prosecution would be pretty certain to drop the case against Pollitt, for it would not want two slaps in the face when one was more than enough. If on the other hand Mann were convicted, it would mean that the atmosphere was strongly against any acquittal for Pollitt, and then Pollitt could defend himself and make a first-class political battle of the case, for he could get away with saying a good many things that I, as a professional lawyer, would not be allowed to say.

When I walked down to the Assize Court on the opening day of trial, I found that the police, no doubt with the agreement of the prosecuting authorities, were trying on some window-dressing. To impress the public, particularly the jury, they had a force of several hundred police all round the Court building, and a large number inside. This was aggressive and dishonest enough, for there was not the slightest danger of disorder; but they committed one more stupid bit of provocation. They decided to exclude all Communists from the public gallery of the Court (as they afterwards admitted, the test they applied to decide whether a man was a Communist was to see if he was poorly dressed, a test which, in the 'thirties, in South Wales, would surely have given the Party a local membership of half a million). This trick, by good fortune, met a judge of icy impartiality, who was not only capable of giving a fair trial to a Communist but had a great belief in the observance of people's rights, including the right to attend a trial. When the complaint of the exclusion of "Communists" was brought to his notice by me just before the case was due to start, we waited nearly twenty minutes before he came into Court; and then he explained exactly what had happened, and said that every citizen, whatever his views, had a right to sit in the gallery so long as he behaved himself, and that he had insisted on those who had been removed by the police being restored to their seats. "There", he concluded, "they will remain as long as they wish, provided they behave themselves."

The hearing could then begin, and the prosecution, conducted for once with scrupulous fairness, proved to be somewhat ridiculous. Not only were the words alleged to have been used scarcely capable of a seditious meaning—indeed, the judge hesitated as to whether he would let the case go to the jury at all—but the police officers who gave evidence as to what Mann had said, and who claimed to have taken it down in shorthand, turned out not even to know what shorthand was, and when they were tested in Court were unable to get down anything at all of what was read out to them. We virtually laughed the case out of Court, and Mann was acquitted. As we expected, the case against Pollitt was then dropped.

The last case with which I deal in this chapter was tried in Canada. Logically, I should deal with it in Chapter 8, below, where I describe some colonial cases; but by the time it happened Canada was no longer a colony in any sense, and indeed was in this matter behaving in a typically imperialist fashion. The case was an astonishing illustration of the way in which a whisper of Communism can lead otherwise intelligent and normally scrupulous people to infringe every rule and principle which they normally boast of observing. I came into the matter personally because I was asked to go to Montreal to take what part I could in the defence of Fred Rose, a Communist member of the Dominion Parliament, charged with espionage.

The background of the case was peculiar. A clerk in the U.S.S.R. Embassy in Ottawa had defected, and told the Royal Canadian Mounted Police, who are now the "security" police organisation of the Dominion, a sensational story of espionage. On this, a tremendous witch-hunt was started throughout Canada, and a large number of alleged spies were prosecuted, almost all of whom were acquitted, to the great credit of various trial judges and juries.

Before any trials could begin, a Royal Commission of two judges of the Supreme Court of Canada, a very eminent Court which has generally done good judicial work, was appointed to enquire into the whole matter. A Commission so composed should have known how to behave, but in fact its work was strongly criticised by lovers of civil liberties on both sides of the Atlantic. For example, in the *Fortnightly Law Journal* of Toronto, Mr. R. M. Willes Chitty wrote:

"The shadow of fear lengthens across the country as the hand of the political police reaches out to snatch men and women from their homes into the concentration camp, uncharged and unaccused, to be held *incomunicado* for inquisition, and perhaps worse, without the benefit of counsel, and denied the cherished right of *Habeas Corpus*, the age-old remedy designed to prevent this very thing."

With or without any legal justification, thirteen people were arrested, detained, kept *incomunicado* for nearly three weeks, cross-examined by the police for many hours, refused access to their legal advisers, and then brought before this Royal Commission, which in effect tried them and found some of them guilty, before they were even charged before any Court that had power to try them. (When one of them, who had been continually demanding to have access to Counsel, asked the Commissioners, after they had finished their examination of him, whether he could now at last have legal assistance, one of them—a Judge of the Supreme Court, remember—said frankly: "I do not know what good Counsel would be to you now.")

The sort of language this Commission used about some of the detained persons was:

> "The evidence established that four persons, namely . . ., have communicated directly or indirectly secret and confidential information to representatives of the U.S.S.R."

Of another person in the same position, they wrote that his refusal "to furnish any explanation and his general demeanour fully convince us that he violated the Official Secrets Act".

This, if you please, was what two eminent judges thought fit to say of people who had never been charged with any offence and were not on trial, but were liable to be so charged and tried before Courts competent to deal with them. One can imagine the difficulties they would have to meet when they ultimately came up for trial before judges and juries who could not be unaware of the fact that these two eminent judges, after what was thought to be a thorough and impartial investigation, had in effect declared them to be guilty of the charges on which they were now to be tried.

After the Commission had in effect found some thirteen people—not including my client Fred Rose, who was never brought before them—guilty of various offences, some of those persons were never even charged at all, presumably because the case against them was too weak; others were charged, and most of them, as I have said, acquitted. In one particularly scandalous instance, after the Commission had pronounced that "there would seem to be no answer on the evidence before us to a charge of conspiring to communicate secret information to an agent of the U.S.S.R.", the man involved was charged with that offence, and the magistrate threw the case out without sending it for trial, on the ground that that there was no evidence against him. The Commission, in their next Report, expressed disagreement with the magistrate, and reasserted their view that he was guilty. He was therefore re-charged, sent for trial, and acquitted.

Fred Rose was in due course charged, tried, and convicted, on weak evidence. I was not able to help him as much as I would have liked, since the Quebec Bar refused to admit me, and the judge refused to hear me unless I was admitted. But I did what I could.

One incident of note in the course of his trial is worth recording, as it throws light on the behaviour of the Royal Commission and on the quiet courage of some of the people concerned. One of the witnesses called by the prosecution in Rose's case was a man who had already been "found guilty" by the Commission; he refused to give evidence, and was told by the judge that if he did not do so he would be sent to prison for contempt of court. "Why", asked the judge, "do you refuse?" He replied very quietly:

> "Because I am going on trial in a short while on similar charges. I have already been tried by the Commission and found guilty. I have already been tried by the newspapers and found guilty. And I do not propose to submit myself to be questioned here so as to help the government in its effort to get me found guilty a third time."

He went to prison for contempt of court, and in due course came up for his own trial. He was acquitted.

Part Two

LAW IN THE COLONIES

5

Colonialism

My second main topic in this book is to discuss the essence—
and the problems—of Colonialism,* so far as concerns the role
of the law and the lawyers in the government of colonial
territories. This is in truth just a crude reproduction of their
role in the metropolitan countries, in the government of the
masses of the people in the interest of the rulers. Even thus
limited to lawyers, the study of colonialism is a large one; the
topic of colonialism as a whole is much larger, and I do not
seek to emulate or copy greater men who have written on the
whole topic. It is, however, impossible to discuss the
legal aspects without writing something about the topic
generally.

What is—or was—a colony? To most readers the word
conveys the idea of a people, generally economically underdeveloped and therefore an easy prey to exploitation, and
generally "coloured", governed by another people, generally
"white", which is more developed, of course capitalist, more
powerful and thus more capable of exploiting others. This
type I call a "direct colony", and it is or was of very frequent
occurrence.

But there are other types, in the political and economic
sense colonial, which should be classified as "indirect colonies"
because nominal sovereignty has not been assumed by the
colonising power, but has been left with the local ruler, while
real power is exercised by the colonialists. There are types
of indirect colony, such as China and Egypt at certain stages
of their history, in which there is little outward sign of their
being colonies, but they are or were just as effectively dominated
as were, say, the Princes' States in India before its independence.

* I use the word Colonialism in preference to Imperialism, as the latter is often
used, and mis-used, in more than one meaning.

F

The essence of all the types is that the lives of the colonial peoples are controlled by the government and ruling class of another, a foreign, people.

Most colonial peoples live in the lands of their origin and their birth, and those who govern them normally have their origins and their permanent homes in other lands. The latter often call the former "natives", almost as if there was something distinctive and unusual in living in one's native land.

In colonialist language, "native" has the further meaning of being a native of a country which is governed by "non-natives", i.e., a colony. It is a correct description of the people concerned, but I do not like to use the word where I can avoid it,* for it has acquired an essentially colonialist secondary meaning, or flavour, of inferiority, subordination, and even inefficiency and limited intelligence, attributed to "natives" by the arrogant colonialists; I shall have to come back to this point. (Whilst I dislike the word, I shall often find it necessary to use it, since there is no other convenient word to describe this important and very numerous section of humanity.)

Among the "direct colonies", taking into account the hard facts rather than the peculiarities of colonialist vocabulary, I include Ireland, which for centuries before its partial liberation half a century ago was in substance, if not in form, a "direct colony", and indeed an acute example of the evils of colonialism. I include British India too, i.e., that part of the Indian sub-continent which—before independence—was under the sovereignty of the "King-Emperor", as distinct from the

---

* For the horrors of the misuse of language, as well as for other and far worse horrors, one can turn to South Africa. When some years ago I visited the abominable "Pass Office" in Johannesburg, where Africans stand and wait for hours and even days to be given—or refused—passes permitting them to exist in certain areas in order to be exploited by the "whites", I saw a sub-division labelled "Foreign Natives". I had always thought of natives as being natives of a country, and of foreigners as being persons not natives of the country, so I asked what "foreign natives" were. It proved to be simple: an African who was a native of some African territory that was not within South Africa was a "native" because he was a black exploitee, and a foreign native because he came to South Africa to be exploited by the whites there.

For light relief, one may turn to a deputation of members of the U.S. House of Representatives who visited Western Europe, including Britain, shortly after the end of the Second World War in order to form an estimate of the economic possibilities of the various countries. They caused wry smiles in this country, not because they thought they could sum us up in a week, but because they described us all in their Report as natives. After all, we were.

"Princes' States" or "Native States". (There were some 600 of these, mostly very small, but a few of them were of great extent, importance, and even wealth. They were never part of the King-Emperor's dominions, but their sovereignty was little more than nominal, real control being in the hands of "British residents", members of the formidably efficient Indian Civil Service, which until a very late stage was exclusively "white".* They were typical "indirect colonies".)

That British India was not normally called a colony— it was always called "India" or "British India"—was only a matter of words. It was a direct colony, just like its neighbour Ceylon, which was always called a colony.

There were other varieties of colonial rule. There were, for example, "protectorates", where not only nominal sovereignty, but sometimes a good deal of real power remained with the original rulers. There was a touch of hypocrisy about the name, for the British, like other colonising Powers, whilst professing to "protect" the inhabitants from other invaders or controllers, were in fact protecting their own economic, strategic and political interests, and were securing the essential advantages of colonialism without the trouble of carrying through a conquest of the territory. Then there were, and indeed here and there still are, "mandated territories", mainly direct colonies of the former German Empire taken from it at the end of the First World War and shared out by the victorious colonialist powers among themselves as—in essence—war booty. The real position of the territories as direct colonies was not altered, but only their masters and the language in which they were ordered about; but hypocrisy—not an exclusive British quality—was allowed a say, in that in the complaisant eyes of international law the territories were not just handed over directly to the takers, but

* The difference between British India and the Princes' States loomed more largely in the minds of many Indians than might have been expected. In Kerala, for example, a State of the Republic of India today, formed almost wholly of the territories of two Princes' States, Travancore and Cochin, both remarkable for having long established and maintained a very high degree of literacy, intelligence and political alertness in lands of terrible poverty, Keralans have often said to me with pride: "Well, at any rate, we were never subjects of the King-Emperor." But to the British establishment the difference was less vivid; earlier in this century, some of the judges of the High Court of Justice at Madras were quite astonished to discover that they could not validly exercise their jurisdiction to hear urgent matters when they were on holiday, because their holiday resort happened to be in a Prince's State.

were nominally put in the hands of the newly-founded League of Nations and entrusted by it, as "mandates", to the various takers who had previously arranged the share-out. These states were to administer the territories on behalf of the League as "trustees"* for the "natives". When the United Nations Organisation was formed after the Second World War, the mandates which still existed were handed over to it.

How little difference there was, in practice and in the eyes of the colonialist power, between a mandated territory and a direct colony can be seen from the proposal put forward by the British government some time ago to amalgamate for its own administrative convenience the three territories of Kenya, Uganda and Tanganyika. The proposal was made without any regard to the fact that Kenya was, whilst in respect of most of its territory a direct colony, a protectorate in respect of its valuable coastal strip, nominally under the sovereignty of the Sultan of Zanzibar, Uganda was a protectorate of a rather "loose" type, in which native kings had a good deal of power, and Tanganyika, which had been German East Africa, was a "mandated territory". The proposal was dropped, but the fact that it was made is a good illustration of the realities of colonial rule, for whatever one may think of the reactionary outlook of the officials of the old Colonial Office, and whatever one may think of their Ministers, one cannot attribute to the officials ignorance of the status of the various territories that lay under their Ministry.

A much more serious and unpleasant reminder of colonialist realities is the case of South-West Africa, a vast area very rich in minerals, taken from the German Empire at the end of the First World War and mandated to South Africa as "trustee". The racist government of the latter country has shown its views of "trust" for "natives" by treating the inhabitants of the territory almost worse than it treats "its own" natives, and has steadily ignored every effort of the United Nations to terminate its mandate and/or to persuade it to treat the inhabitants better.

These varieties of colonial rule cover, I think, the whole field

---

* It is odd that the notion of "trusts" should be applied, for the essence of trusts in English law—the system that originated trusts—is that the trustee may never directly or indirectly make a profit out of the trust.

that I have to consider in this chapter, but if one is to have a full picture of all treatments of one people by another which are in essence colonial, one must study two other capitalist activities.

The first of these lies in the treatment, within the territories of any developed state, of peoples who are economically weaker —often partly through racial differences—than the dominant people of the state, such as the Irish in England, the Moslems in some areas of British India before independence, coloured peoples in the U.S.A., and of recent years Asian and West Indian immigrants in Britain. Such a position arises whenever one group has a markedly lower standard of living, or has had little opportunity to acquire useful skills or has less ability to adjust itself to a different "way of life". I do not need to give detailed consideration to this problem here, as it has no immediate relevance to the role of law and lawyers in colonial territories, but it is in my view necessary to see something of its nature if one is to have a full grasp of the character of colonialism, and so to understand the role of laweyrs, or of anyone else, in the colonies.

All the activities of colonialists are in truth just crude manifestations and developments of capitalist practice in the metropolitan countries, i.e., of the exploitation of man by man which capitalism operates whenever and wherever—and with whatever harshness will best serve the "cause" of private profit— it has the opportunity. Once it operated in the "dark satanic mills" of early industrial England, today in speeded-up modern factories with conveyor-belts, and further afield, in colonies, by taking super-profits from very cheap "native" labour on fertile lands, paid at incredibly low rates.*

* In the 'fifties of this century, some Labour members of Parliament exposed the case of a Kenya settler who was paying 30s. a month to his adult skilled African workers in the fertile "White Highlands" (called White because only Whites could hold land there, although Africans could work for them on their farms) and making colossal profits thereby. I was amused to be told in Kenya at the time that it was not quite "fair" to have selected this particular settler for criticism, since he paid his workers more than some other settlers. (And if it be put forward as an excuse that the Africans were not highly-skilled, I recall that one settler showed me with justifiable pride that by the use of a bulldozer he had altered the flow of a stream to turn several acres of swamp into good arable land. I asked him who had actually worked the bulldozer, and he said: "One of my Africans." And, when I asked how long it had taken to teach the man to work it, he replied: "An hour or two.")

The colonialists who thus exploit the "natives" are economically speaking the descendants of the capitalists who made super-profits out of the slave-trade, both collecting, shipping and selling the slaves, and in the exploitation of slaves on the American plantations; and then, when the exploitation of "free labour" was found to be more profitable, nobly gave up their slave-holding and received large sums by way of compensation.

Today, or perhaps I should say until yesterday, the exploitation of native labour had the advantage of being almost free of any criticism or control by public opinion, for the only effective public opinion in the average colony was that of the exploiters and of other whites with similar outlooks; they had the advantage, too, of dealing with workers with little experience of negotiating with white employers, and with no effective trade union to help them.

The second of the two manifestations of capitalism in colonial territories which I mentioned above is that of "neo-colonialism". I must not deal with it in great detail, for by its very nature it calls for no work by colonialist lawyers "on the ground", and does not involve the direct administration of one people's country by members of another people. The essence of neo-colonialism lies in the attempt—too often highly successful —by ex-colonial powers to secure by economic and financial pressure on newly-independent ex-colonies the profits which they formerly enjoyed under "direct" rule. It is operated mainly by the financial control of the industries in the new state, which are naturally enough wholly or partly owned by "metropolitan" capitalists, by the extraction of vast sums for repayment of or interest on old and new loans, and by the control of world market prices which enables the neo-colonialists both to reduce the receipts the neo-colonialised country can get for its raw material exports, and to raise the price it must pay for the imports it needs.

The facts thus contradict all the cunning capitalist propaganda that has gone on over the years, the "virtues" of the colonial system. According to this propaganda, the colonial territories have been and still are unselfishly administered by a succession of capitalist governments and enterprises in the interests of the inhabitants, who have greatly benefited by getting roads and railways, by obtaining employment, and by various other advantages.*

I must still write a little more about colonialism generally before I deal directly with the role of the lawyers. I begin with a fact that surprises many who know little more about the colonial system than they have been able to learn from that section of the press which serves the interest of a tiny section of the nation, and is quaintly called "national", namely that at the height of the colonial period, say just before the beginning of the Second World War, the area affected by colonialism was of immense extent, indeed more than half of the inhabited world. Direct rule covered a large part of Asia, nearly all Africa,† and the West Indies. As for indirect colonies, they covered all of Latin America and China. Until 1917, they included half of Tsarist Russia too.

It is not surprising, once one understands the basis of colonialism, that the area affected was so large. For the opportunity and the consequent temptation—irresistible to capitalists—to colonise arose whenever and wherever rich and developed capitalist countries, always needing new fields for the investment of their surpluses, could see undeveloped territories whose rulers and peoples could offer little effective resistance to conquest and exploitation. The natural resources and potentially available labour force of these territories provided the means of acquiring vast quantities of raw materials very cheaply, and promised at the same time markets for manufactured goods. It was generally just a matter of economic convenience whether such tempting booty should become direct or indirect colonies; the governing consideration was how cheaply and firmly control could be gained of territories and

* In the Parliament of 1935-45, on one occasion when colonial matters were under discussion, I watched the lovable and highly-educated William Gallacher, sitting by my side, growing more and more restive whilst a string of aged and mentally rather limited Tories chattered about the noble work which the British were unselfishly doing as trustees for the natives. At last he could remain silent no longer, and contributed a salient point to the discussion by ejaculating: "Trustees? Burglars, ye mean!"

† I say, "nearly all", for Ethiopia should be regarded as not being colonial except for the short period when fascist Italy conquered and held it. I remember that when Mussolini started to invade, the late Lord Ponsonby, an aristocrat with a clear understanding and hatred of colonialism, remarked: "The fool! Can he not understand that, if there had been any prospect of profit in taking that country, the British would have done so long ago?"

people before other gangs of capitalists could grab them. In most cases, conquest seemed quick and secure, and the loss of life involved, including that of the troops of the invaders, did not worry the colonialists.*

It is not necessary for me to study in any detail the various means employed to acquire colonies, for they are almost irrelevant to the problems of lawyers in administering the colonies once they are acquired. One typical instance of colonialist disregard of the interests of the conquered people, may be noted, however. When the various colonising powers had finished their seizure of territories, and had settled—by force or by discussion—the boundaries between their respective territories, it was found that these boundaries took no account of national, racial or tribal frontiers, but often ran right through the middle of groups of peoples, who thus found themselves not merely conquered but arbitrarily divided from their neighbours and relatives by frontiers bearing no relation to their histories but merely to the relative military strengths of their competing conquerors.† Such considerations did not weigh with the conquerors, but they have caused and still cause distress and trouble to many colonial peoples, and no doubt aid the "divide and rule" tactics of the whites.

* So little were they conscious of anything shameful or inhuman in their activities that I noticed once that in the time-tables of the Burmese Railways, which were read by literate Burmese as well as by the whites, a prominent place near the beginning, which in Europe might have been occupied by an advertisement for holiday resorts, was given to a pretty long list—not particularly essential to finding one's train—of the series of wars which the British had undertaken in order to conquer Burma.

† Kwame Nkrumah, for example, who long led the peoples of Ghana, was a member of a tribe whose lands were thus divided. Had he been born in the same tribe a few miles further West, he would have been governed by the French in the Ivory Coast, would have spoken French, and would presumably have led a successful anti-colonial struggle against the French instead of against the British.

6

Principles of Colonial Rule

I now examine the principles and attitudes of colonial powers in the government of their colonies. Basically, they have been greedy, racialist, and arrogant.

I take first the non-economic, or at least not primarily and patently economic, bases of their attitudes. Here the first and most outstanding feature was and is the assumption that all "natives"—whether African peasants cultivating their lands by primitive methods, or Indians steeped in the elaborate social, political and cultural traditions of their infinitely varied peoples (many of whom had been highly civilised when the ancestors of the "superior" colonialists were painting their bodies with woad)—are naturally and inevitably inferior in culture, capacities and intelligence to their white "masters", and incapable of rising to the latters' level even if anyone were foolish enough to try to raise them.

By now, in any area of thought to the left of the lunatic fringe of the Tory Party (or just possibly that of right-wing Labour), it is part of "the common currency of thought", to borrow a phrase from Winston Churchill, that this assumption of basic "native" inferiority is nonsense. But this nonsense has operated throughout the centuries and decades of colonialism in aid of any amount of capitalism's dirty work, and we must see how it has applied. It is no more than an extra aggravation of the white "superiority" imposture that most of the white personnel in the colonies (with the important exception of India) were not even good members of the British ruling class—not that it itself was remarkable for outstanding cultural or education development; those who went to the colonies were in the main "second rate" men or "rejects" in the sense that they sought employment in the colonies because they were not able to secure or hold good posts in their home country. This was especially the case among

lawyers, to whom I will come in Chapter 8. But, in spite of
the relatively poor quality of most of the personnel, the cunning
of the ruling class, operating through the able civil servants
in the Colonial Office in London, with the advantages of long
experience in "managing" colonial peoples and of the financial
and administrative grip on the territories, enabled the system
to maintain itself pretty well until after the Second World War.

In the administration, the assumption of the inferiority of
"natives", which I have described above, had wide and
terrible effects, administratively, socially, commercially, industrially, agriculturally, and of course in the law itself.
Administratively, for many decades—and in the case of India
for centuries—no native was regarded as capable of doing any
but the simplest—and of course the most poorly-paid—work.
This prejudice was very slowly broken down, especially in
India, where by the time independence was won probably more
than half of the judges of the High Courts* were Indians;
and much the same development occurred in other branches
of the Indian administration. (As a variant, with the added
feature of resort to "divide and rule" which I shall discuss a
little later, one saw in colonies such as Kenya, where there was
a substantial population of Indians, that "medium" posts were
given to Indians, and only minor ones went to Africans.)

Socially, until very recently, even in British India, there was
an almost complete colour bar. No "white" would receive any
native in his house, except of course native servants,† or enter

* In English legal language, a Court that is called "High" is an important
Court, generally with unlimited jurisdiction, but Courts that are called "Supreme"
are more important still. In India, until shortly before independence, there was
never any all-India Court, and all the Courts were courts of the Provinces, or even
of smaller areas. This was done as part of the policy of keeping the various Provinces separate, and having the minimum of central government, so as to combat
such anti-colonialist sentiment as was able to develop, by giving it no national core
round which it could build. So the High Courts there were, the highest Courts there were,
but each of them had its being and jurisdiction only within its Province. (From the
lawyers' point of view, the development of the law at its highest level was aided—
and very well aided—by providing appeals from all the High Courts to the Privy
Council in London; see Chapter 7 of Book 2.)

† This employment of native domestic servants produced an almost comic
situation in Nairobi in the 'fifties. A new cinema was opened, and announced that
Africans would not be admitted. Protests followed from white women, who were
accustomed to send their young children to the cinemas in charge of their African
servants (who ranked as unfit for social contact with whites but as suitable guardians of their children). The owners of the cinema had to issue a modified announcement to the effect that Africans would not be admitted unless they were in the
company of white children.

the house of a native, except the very highest. As for inter-marriage—which was quite common and devoid of social stigma in most French colonies, whose governments were in general neither better nor worse than the British—any white man who took courage to marry a "native"—perhaps a Kashmiri lady of the standing, say, of Nehru's daughter Indira Gandhi—was immediately subjected to the same colour bar, in effect a social boycott. (The sexual bar was similar; in many colonies it was a criminal offence for a native to have connection with a white woman, although white men were not embarrassed by corresponding legislation.)

Commercially, natives would normally work only in sub-ordinate positions.* There would be no direct prohibition of their carrying on business on their own account, but in most colonies—not in India—they would generally be unable to secure premises, finance or credit to make it practicable for them to do so. (In Kenya, where most shops were kept by Indians, Africans could in practice only run "African shops", which only Africans frequented, and where only goods of poor quality, which Africans could afford to buy, were on sale.)

Industrially, no native could be employed in any but the simplest and most poorly-paid jobs, however able he might be.† In South Africa, for example, it was and is unlawful for natives to be employed in any but the most humble position, and if any were found to be engaged in more important work their passes would be withdrawn and they would have to go back to their villages. When I was in Johannesburg, a progressive white manager of an industrial plant introduced me to an African who was in fact the foreman of an important department in the factory; the man had to be listed and paid as an unskilled

* When I was able to visit Johannesburg in the 'fifties (with the result that I was honoured by being afterwards listed as an "undesirable immigrant") a white friend sent his office boy with me to show me the way to another friend. The "boy" was an African of about forty years, and as we started I tried to think of something to talk with him about, since plainly I could not just walk in silence with him. He saved me the trouble by saying at once: "I am very happy to meet you, for I always read your articles in *Labour Monthly*."

† When I visited Rumania shortly after the Second World War, I found an interesting parallel. Rumania had been almost an indirect colony of Germany, and still more of certain great oil concerns. When with the help of the Soviet Union the oilfields were nationalised, it was found that the previous owners had never employed any Rumanian to do much more than turn taps on and off.

worker, and the balance of his real wages was handed to
him secretly.

As for industrial activity carried on by natives on their own
account, even on a small scale, there were few colonies—India
apart—where it was possible for them to run more than handi-
crafts or one- or two-man workshops.

Agriculturally—and in almost all colonies the great majority
of the people worked on the land—their fate varied from colony
to colony, according to the whites' need for land, or the need to
drive people from the villages to work in mines or industries,
or the nature of the soil. Generally, the natives lost their land
and, if they did not go to the towns or mines, had to farm
inferior land or to work for miserable wages for whites on
the good land, cultivating not the crops they wanted or
needed, but those which were profitable for the new white
landowners.

In the law, until a pretty late stage in colonial history, it
was generally the rule that only barristers (or sometimes also
solicitors) with British qualifications could practise in any
colony, a provision not perhaps unreasonable in early days,
when the only lawyers would be British, and would naturally
qualify in Britain; but in the period when natives wanted to
qualify, this rule imposed the almost impossible burden that
the native would have to go to England, stay there several
years to study and qualify, maintain himself meanwhile, and
pay his admission fees. Some less poor natives managed this;
but in Kenya, for example, when I went out in 1952 to defend
Kenyatta (to whose case I will return in Chapter 9) there was
only one qualified African lawyer in the whole country, and he
had only just been called and had not started to practice.
(Kenyatta was defended by one European (myself), one
Kenya Indian, one Kenya Goan, and one Nigerian, with
occasional help from another European, an Indian, and a West
Indian.)

The colour bar, closely linked with most of the matters which
I have been discussing needs a little separate discussion. In
effect, it marked off all peoples whose skin was not "white"
from those with "white" skins, as if they were not wholly
human, and were certainly not entitled to the same rights or
consideration as whites in any human relation or activity,

even when they were allowed to fight and die on behalf of the whites in their wars. Much of what I have written above is illustrative of this situation, but there is further material which I should mention about it. For example, it was a commonplace of colonial life, including Indian, that any seat or place where a native had been had to be swept clean before it was used by a white; if, for example, any Indian had to attend at some office before a white official, the area where he had stood or sat would be cleaned after he had left. (I knew of one grotesque example involving an Indian who—not long before independence—had reached a high position in the Indian Civil Service. He was one of the not too rare type of educated Indian who became so fanatically pro-British that they adopted the colour bar, with themselves on the white side. And he made it a practice to have his office swept—of course by an Indian sweeper—whenever an Indian had been in there before him.)

The same revolting and un-Christian attitude affected many of the Christian churches. When I expressed my pleasure on being told in Zanzibar that a particular church was shared by white and native Christians, my informant went on to explain that the two colours did not actually worship God in the one church *at one and the same time*, but that the natives had a separate service fairly early in the day, after which the church was swept. It was clear from what he told me that even this was an advance on the general practice that whites and natives should worship the same God in wholly separate buildings. Some churches actually taught that the colour bar and the inferiority of coloured people was God's teaching.

The manifestations of the colour bar made me so angry when I met them "on the ground" in all their crudity that I do not regret in the least what I recall as perhaps the rudest thing I ever said. I was walking in the early part of the day in a beautiful part of Kerala, looking at the sun in the trees, and at a string of monkeys swinging from tree to tree in long graceful leaps; and there were a group of Keralans sitting in the shade reading newspapers (in itself unusual in India except in Kerala, for only there is the bulk of the population literate). An English gentleman, in the khaki shorts and shirt of the old conquerors, looked at the Keralans, and then remarked to me—assuming, which always maddened me, that I would share his abominable views—"They're just down from the trees, I suppose."* This stung me into the retort: "Well, that will leave more room for you."

The colour-bar is not just humanly revolting; it lies at the root of innumerable atrocities such as those perpetrated by Americans, for example, on the natives of Korea and Vietnam. It is easier to torture and murder people if you can begin by persuading yourself that they are not fully human.

The colour bar has its smaller and sillier consequences, too. For example, some years ago, in Kenya, a young African employed as a caddy on a golf course, who occasionally borrowed some clubs and played a few holes "on the quiet", was discovered to be a real golfing genius. Considerable efforts were made by a number of people, whites included, to make arrangements that would somehow enable him to play golf, and perhaps to become as famous as some of the Kenyan long-distance runners, but it proved to be impossible.

The policy of "divide and rule" is another matter which deserves a little consideration; it is not of course solely a colonialist policy, but is well-adapted to colonial problems. The policy was first worked out by one of the earliest and greatest colonialists, Julius Caesar; the translation of his Latin: "Divide et impera" gave rise to a "schoolboy-howler", when it was translated as "dividends and empire". The essence of the policy is that anyone exercising power can gain greatly in strength if he can somehow divide up the people whom he wishes to dominate and get them to quarrel with one another instead of uniting in revolt against him. In the industrial struggle in this country, it is often used or attempted to be used by concessions made to one group of workers in the hope that they will not be ready to come out on strike in support of another group. And it has more obvious applications in colonial territories, where there are ready-made or easily-created differences between, for example, two races (Indians and Africans in Kenya), two religions (Hindus and Moslems in British India), or even peoples of strikingly different standards of living, such as the English and Irish in some areas of England.

I will give a few examples, starting with the Hindu-Moslem

---

* It is part of the "folk-lore" of the colour-barsters that all coloured people are so uncivilised that they can be regarded as only about one generation removed from apes.

conflict in British India. This was and is often explained by supporters of colonialism as an inevitable and as it were self-generated mutual religious antagonism, easily understood by many people in Britain who, as one Irish bishop put it, find it easy to hate each other for the love of God. But in truth it was in most areas of British India and at most periods deliberately fomented as an invaluable weapon of the astonishingly efficient administration of the Indian Empire by the highly-trained élite of the Indian Civil Service. The crudest example of its actual operation that has come to my notice was that of a friend of mine who some thirty or forty years ago was made the head of a university in India where the staff and the students were in part Hindu and in part Moslem. On his appointment, he had stipulated that he was to have a free hand to suppress any manifestation of Hindu-Moslem antagonism among either the staff or the students. He had not been in his post very long when he received evidence of deliberate fostering of religious hatred among the students by one of the professors. He challenged the latter, who frankly admitted his conduct, and said that he proposed to continue it. My friend had power to dismiss him instantly, and did so. The professor grinned, and walked out; and within an hour or two the Collector* of the district strode into my friend's office in a towering rage, with a revolver in each hand, and asked him if he had indeed dismissed the professor. He said he had, and the Collector replied:

"How on earth do you imagine I can keep order in my district if I don't keep the Hindus and the Moslems in conflict with one another? You must reinstate the professor immediately."

This, of course, my friend refused to do, and in a short time he was dismissed himself, the professor was reinstated, the Hindu-Moslem conflict was maintained, "order" was restored, and —in the longer run—British India ceased to exist.

Another and very different example is to be found 120 years ago, at the time of what we have been taught to call the "Indian Mutiny", and Indians generally call the Great Rebellion. This would almost have succeeded if the British had not been able to persuade some of the rich Indian communities, mainly in the

* "Collectors" were British officials who substantially speaking governed small districts; they were not unlike the District Commissioners in many Crown Colonies. The name "Collector" was a frank expression of the fact that an important part of their work was to collect revenue.

Province of Bombay, in return for substantial concessions, to oppose the rebellion and refuse its leaders financial aid.

There was an unusual, and in some ways particularly unpleasant, sample of "divide and rule" in recent years in the case of Cyprus. This island, predominantly Greek in population, with a dwindling Turkish minority, was long a Turkish colony, which was leased by Turkey to Britain in 1878 and then annexed by Britain in the First World War, when Turkey joined in on Germany's side. Until quite recently, there was very little conflict between Greek Cypriots and Turkish Cypriots, the two communities living peaceably side by side in nearly all towns and villages. The Government of Turkey never attempted to interfere, and one could feel pretty certain that the British government would have rejected any such interference. But when, after the Second World War, it became clear that on the one hand Cyprus would claim independence and on the other that owing to its geographical position it had become of great strategic importance to the Middle East interests of Britain, which had lost its hold on the Egyptian ports and had no secure ports in Greece, Britain began to stir up antagonism between the Turkish and Greek Cypriots, and in particular to bring the Turkish government into the scene as a protector of the Turkish Cypriots, in order to weaken the fight for independence and to secure bases for itself even if independence resulted. The result was that there were bitter racial conflicts, and for years a civil war, in the formerly peaceful island, so that, when it became independent, it was unable to refuse the British demand for an "independent" military and Air Force base in the island, and that the peaceful and efficient administration of the island, in the face of a now antagonistic Turkish minority given great power to disrupt the business of government under the Constitution, became almost impossible.

In many African colonies, differences between the substantial numbers of tribes which inhabit them have been maintained and exacerbated by the British rulers as a simple and easy method of "dividing and ruling", into which I need not go in detail. But I should mention one colonial policy, not the same thing as "divide and rule", namely that of "chiefs' rule". Among many African peoples, before colonisation, chiefs were a genuine and important part of their government; sometimes hereditary and sometimes popularly elected, they were the real rulers and leaders of a tribe, and sometimes of a nation. In some colonies, the British rulers adopted, or purported to adopt, the "chief system", but in fact under this system the chiefs were appointed and paid by the government, which dismissed them if they turned out to be "unco-operative". The chiefs were thus no more than agents of the colonial government appointed to rule districts on its behalf. I had a glimpse of the reality of their position at the trial of Kenyatta. I called as a defence witness a chief who seemed to me a man of honesty and intelligence, willing to give evidence of facts which helped my client. I did not know how much risk he was taking, but I saw that he was a useful witness for my client, and so called him. This led to the prosecutor asking me quietly whether the man was really a chief, and I said that he was. The prosecutor, with a frankness that I think stemmed simply from his being so accustomed to the government punishing people for giving evidence against it (and thus, in truth, committing contempt of its own Courts), said: "Yes, he seems to be a chief, but he won't be one much longer." And the man was dismissed within a week. (We shall see a much grosser case of ill-treatment of a chief for giving evidence against the government when I recount in Chapter 9 the trial of Julius Nyereri in Tanganyika.)

A minor variant of "divide and rule" arises when troops or police are or may have to be used against popular movements or popular individuals. In the Kenyatta case, although the trial was held in a remote area, where the primitive inhabitants had probably never been allowed to hear of Kenyatta, the government still had the problem of guarding him and his five co-accused both in the prison and on their way to and from the courtroom. Whites were too expensive to be used for all this work, and men recruited anywhere in the more populous parts of Kenya would very likely know and admire Kenyatta; so the government used a very old device, recruiting prison guards from Somaliland.* Not long after the

---

* This is paralleled by the British practice, in the days when troops were used to maintain "law and order" in times of industrial unrest, of using troops enlisted in other districts, for preference agricultural ones, far from that in which they were to be used.

trial began, one of these Somalis said to one of the Kenya Africans around the prison: "I am going to desert and return to my own country. They told me when they engaged me to come here that I was to guard criminals, but I can see that these men are not criminals but chiefs. I will not be used to guard such men." And he duly deserted.

Another serious evil of colonialism was the distortion or destruction—in the service of capitalist profit-seeking—of the whole way of life of the colony—feudal or pre-feudal, as dear to the natives as their own way of life is to any other people, but "inconvenient" to the whites since it was ill-adapted to modern methods of the exploitation of man by man. Distortion was achieved by a whole series of operations, particularly in relation to taxation and land-law. The immediate object was to adapt the native population, by whatever degree of compulsion might be necessary, to serve the interests of the dominant power, as labour force in mines or in factories or in large-scale cultivation of land for cash crops, and—where natives were left to continue working on the land—to secure by land laws and by administrative measures that the system of landholding should be well adapted to white ideas of cultivation and to making taxation easy of collection (and, where the need arose, to the adjustment of taxation so as to drive some of the population off the land and into industry).

As for the land laws, it was the most natural thing in the world from the English point of view—and convenient too, for taxation and for expropriation—that all land should be owned individually by some identifiable (and taxable) person. To many colonial peoples this was strange and even repugnant, for their land would often belong to families, or extended families, or to a village community or other bodies which meant much to them. Every time the two interests clashed, the whites won, and the distortion grew sharper—and, in the long run, the movement for independence grew.

Similarly, decisions on the development of the colony, and the carrying-out of those decisions, were the work of the whites, done as they thought most useful for the interests they served. Minerals would be sought for, won, or left in the ground, as best served those interests, which were seeking profits not only in that colony but elsewhere. In agriculture they decided what should be grown—it might be ground-nuts, cotton, cocoa, tea, or something else profitable—regardless of the wishes, habits or true interests of the natives. One of the horrors of this was the creation of "one-crop economies" such as Egypt and the Sudan, which were put to grow cotton; such countries were dependent on the world-market price of their product, which could be largely dictated by the powerful monopolies, and could ruin a whole colony—or be used to "bring it to heel". Of course, the best land available in the colony would be used for the crops the whites and their governments wanted to grow, and the natives on that land would in part be "absorbed" as landless labour to cultivate the newly chosen crops, and in part given poorer land, inadequate in quality and extent to afford them a reasonable life.

The whole business of recruiting labour for all the developments decided on by the whites was another elaborate department of the distortion. It was "necessary" to ensure that sufficient labour should be forthcoming, and to fix rates of wages for the workers at, of course, the lowest rates which—with whatever pressure could be brought to bear—the men would accept. Sometimes, the various upheavals of colonial life, or the growth of the population, would give a fairly large supply of labour; but if it was necessary to increase the supply, a favourite weapon was the poll-tax. In most colonies, the population had not formerly lived in a "money economy", had little need of money in ordinary life, and had very little of this strange commodity. If a poll-tax of only a few shillings a year on each member of a family were imposed, it would present a burden so great that nearly every peasant family had to send off at least one of its adult male members to the towns or the mines or the industries in order to earn the shillings required to meet the tax; and thus the government got not only revenue but a steady stream of new labour. Thus were families broken up, and the interests of capitalist development served. (I was amused a few years ago to listen to the complaints of a Frenchman who had spent some years in one of the French possessions in the South Seas, where the natives, who could live off the land with very little work, were so "stupid"—as he put it—that they would not work for the whites, even for "good" wages, and "more intelligent" natives had to be imported from other islands to do the work that the whites held to be necessary. He was, politically and economically, a cousin of the earnest young white civil servant in Kenya who told me that the poverty of the natives was their own fault because they refused to acquire "good industrial habits".)

When labour was available, its wages had of course to be fixed by "negotiation" between the government or large employers on the one side and the inexperienced natives on the other, who formed a new proletariat, and were for a long time without any trade unions. The formation of unions moved very slowly, naturally enough with variations from one colony to another; but the colonial governments step by step allowed them to be formed, under legislation which made registration —which the government could grant or refuse at its discretion —essential to the legality of the union. A favourite step was to grant registration only to small local unions—the equivalent in our terms of branches—and thus to prevent the creation of any large union, let alone a Trade Union Congress. A little later came the apparently substantial forward step of appointing "labour advisers", whites recruited in Britain. The only ones I actually met were so "safe" that they would have seemed to be impossibly right-wing even in the most right-wing circles of the Labour and trade union movement in Britain. Even with all these disadvantages, the industrial workers in some colonies would at times go on strike, and at a pretty early stage in the strike the police or troops would shoot down strikers, in the name of "law and order", and be duly exonerated by a government enquiry.*

I can give some illustration from Kenya of the way land cultivation worked out in the interests of the whites as against the natives. One example is the case of the famous "White Highlands", so called because only whites could farm them and because they were "high" in the sense that they lay between

---

* The habit of shooting demonstrators was deeply engrained in the authorities in many colonies, and above all in British India, where naturally industries and industrial workers and unions were present on a far greater scale than elsewhere. I once had an argument with a high police official of the government of independent India, who had been trained in the police of British India. He argued sincerely and almost with passion that by far the most humane way to deal with demonstrators was to shoot at once, as that led to fewer deaths in the long run. (This treatment would of course still be given to demonstrators in Britain if they had not long ago grown too strong in the class struggle to allow it.)

7,000 and 10,000 feet above sea level. They had a beautiful climate, straddling the Equator at that altitude, and good soil. What was the position of a native of Kenya who wanted to cultivate land in the White Highlands—who or whose family had perhaps done so for years? The answer was simple; he was not allowed to do so. He could work there as a farm-labourer for 30s. a month or less, but he could not own any land there, or cultivate it for himself. It was reserved for whites, and for a long time the prohibition was additionally aggravating in that much of the land was not being actually cultivated at all, but was just waiting until some white settler should come and take it up. (By a touch of hypocrisy, there was no law expressly forbidding Africans to take up land in the White Highlands, but just one forbidding anyone to do so unless he obtained a licence from a Government Board; and only whites could get licences.)

Next, when an African had some land to cultivate, however poor or cramped, he was still not free to decide for himself what crops he should grow. Coffee, for example, which showed fantastic profits—one English settler whom I knew made a clear profit on one year's crop of £70,000 after tax—was prohibited for Africans on the pretext that, if they were allowed to grow coffee, it might be diseased. But, of course, they could grow maize, the staple food of most of the natives; and they had the apparent advantage that a government Marketing Board was bound to buy all the maize they might grow and to pay a guaranteed price for the grade of maize into which it divided all the maize delivered to it. Surely, that was all right? But there was still a disadvantage; the guaranteed price for maize differed greatly according to the colour of the skin of the grower. Two bags of maize might be identical in grade, and in all other respects; but one grown by a white settler (i.e., grown for him by his African labour on lands which had belonged to them or their families or their ancestors and now belonged to the settler) received a very much larger price than the other one, grown by a native, perhaps with more effort and on poorer soil. It is not surprising that Africans would often tell the story: "When the English came to our country, we had the land, and they had only the Bible. They taught us to pray, and told us that we ought to close our eyes while we prayed. We did so, and when we opened our eyes again we found that they had the land and we had only the Bible."*

Another example from Kenya dates from a little further back. In the 'thirties, after a dispute about the right of a tribe or sub-tribe called Kavirondo to occupy certain lands, they were placed in occupation and given a solemn government under-taking that they would never be disturbed in their occupation. Not long afterwards the government told them they would have to give the land up after all, as it had been found to be rich in gold. They naturally resisted, and the matter was presented to the British public by its press as one more example of the folly and impracticability of this "primitive" people, unable even to understand that an important thing like gold must override both the rights of the tribe and the pledged word of the govern-ment. (There was of course no suggestion that the gold be-longed to the tribe who owned the land, as would have been the legal position in England.)

When I was in Kenya in the fifties, I asked what had been the result of the dispute, which had seemed to die quietly in our press. At first, no one could recall anything about it, but finally an older man was able to tell me that, after all the bother, the all-wise whites had found that there was no workable quantity of gold under the land.

There were other examples of what one might call industrial or agricultural preferences as between peoples. One of the longest established was probably the case of Ireland, where for centuries no substantial industries were allowed to develop lest they should interfere with the profits of English industrial-ists. The only exception—based emphatically on the colonialist idea of "divide and rule"—was the specially-favoured "planta-tions" of Scotsmen in Ulster, introduced in the seventeenth century as a means of holding down the rebellious Irish.

Similar preferences were to be seen in British India. For many years, cotton was grown in India, shipped to England, and there spun and woven into cotton cloth, much of it being sent

* It may surprise English lawyers to learn that, at the trial of Kenyatta to which I will come on Chapter 9, a trial held under the strict English law of evidence, it was ruled by the magistrate that evidence could be given that Kenyatta had allegedly told this story at a public meeting, in order to establish the charge that Kenyatta was a member of the illegal organisation called Mau Mau. The line of reasoning was that Mau Mau was anti-British, the story was anti-British, and therefore anyone who told it was Mau Mau.

back to India to be sold to Indians. Thus, profits were made for the English at each stage. After a time, Indian capitalists began to set up cotton mills in their own country, so as to make cotton cloth out of Indian cotton and supply it to Indian workers. This led to powerful demands in England that the British government of India should prohibit the production of cotton cloth in India in order to protect the profits of English mill-owners (and the employment of English cotton operatives). A long battle followed, which for a time led to the limitation of the amounts of cloth which could be permitted to be produced in India. And finally independence put an end to it all.

I saw a smaller, but significant example, when I went to Uganda for the first time. There the peasants, although poor enough, were far less poor than the Kenyans from among whom I had just come, and their womenfolk could afford to dress in gaily coloured cotton cloth. I congratulated my friends on this, and they replied: "Yes, it is good as far as it goes. We can afford them, but we have to pay three or four times as much for them as we would if we could buy them from Japan. The government insists on their coming from England."

7

The Framework of Government in Colonies

The framework of government in colonies is an important tool of the despotic control of colonial peoples in the interest of the dominant power. It has of course varied greatly from colony to colony and from period to period. Some colonies which were taken by conquest, and already had a well-developed government apparatus, such as Quebec and Guyana, were taken over with that apparatus kept largely intact. In some, especially protectorates, much of the standing apparatus was maintained, with some overlay of the British colonial system. And a few were governed by what used to be called "indirect rule", where much of the administration was entrusted to "reliable" chiefs, without even much introduction of English law or English Courts. But in most colonies the "native" system of government bore no resemblance to any European system, and was ill-adapted to the needs of a colonialist government desirous of ruling with a strong executive, and more or less dictatorially.

In that great majority of cases, the colonialists set up a purely British-type apparatus, with a Governor at the head (and, in the case of a large territory that might be divided into provinces, with Lieutenant-Governors over the provinces), and in all cases with District Commissioners ruling large districts. The rule would be generally absolute. In the early days, laws would be made by the "Governor in Council", which would mean the Governor and a small group of high officials; and then, in most colonies, as they became more developed—and as the native agitation for a greater share in their own government and later for independence grew—there would be a Legislative Council with, say, about one-third of its members "popularly" elected on a very narrow franchise, the remainder being officials plus perhaps members nominated by the Governor. Ultimately the stage would be reached at which all the members save three or four officials would be elected, on a franchise rather wider than before, but generally with property or educational qualifications or other provisions designed to ensure that whites should have at least one hundred times the representation conceded to the natives.*

Even in colonies where some measure of self-government, or at least some relaxation of unrestricted despotism, had been conceded, the aura of sacrosanctity which surrounded even District Commissioners was such that governments were reluctant to put them into the witness-box if there was any risk of their being competently cross-examined and accused of not telling the truth. This may have been part of the reason why at the trial of Nyereri in Tanganyika, which I shall describe in Chapter 9, the prosecution took the curious course of not calling either of the two District Commissioners directly involved.

What might fairly be called the Constitution of any colony sufficiently developed to have such an instrument was generally enshrined in an "Order in Council" made by the British government in London. Historically, such an Order was a formal act of the executive made by the King (or Queen) in his (or her) Privy Council. Today it is in reality just a way of expressing the decision of the government.

The Constitution thus made would often provide that further constitutional matters could be dealt with by Ordinances† made in the colony by the Governor in Council (corresponding roughly, in the nineteenth and twentieth centuries, to the "King in Council" of earlier times).

A special feature of the work of government—in reality but not in form—in most colonies was the missionaries, who worked in missions set up by various Christian churches to impart Christianity to Moslem (or, in India, also Hindu and

---

* Some colonies never got as far as having any elected members at all. For example, the legislative council of the rich and important colony of Hong Kong has not and never has had any but official and nominated members, and there was some amusement and embarrassment there a few years ago, when an American "statesman" visited the colony and made a speech saying how happy he felt to get away from the "Communist dictatorship" of the Peoples' Republic of China and breathe the free air of a democracy governed by a freely and popularly elected legislature.

† "Ordinance" was the title normally given to local legislative measures until the stage was reached when a Legislative Council had substantial resemblance to an elected Parliament, when its measures might be called Acts.

Buddhist) or pagan natives, and were staffed by white missionaries (with, one trusts, the hope that the natives would not
see too clearly the contrasts between Christian principles and
the actions of their nominally Christian rulers). Either as an
extra and independent activity, or as a valuable means of
making their missions more acceptable to the natives, or out
of sheer Christian goodwill (or a combination of some or all
of these), the missionaries gave the natives some elementary
education, whereas they would otherwise receive none, or very
little, and some medical care. (It would come only at a later
stage that educational and medical service would be given by
the colonial government.) The missionaries thus rendered the
natives valuable aid,* and some of them were very fine people.
But it must not be forgotten that they had to conform, and did
conform, with the outlook and the demands of the colonialist
governments. They could teach the natives to "fear God", but
they had to be sure to teach them also to "honour the King",
in whose name the whole profitable horror of colonialism was
inflicted on them, and to honour and obey those who ruled
them in the King's name. By giving teaching—on the "right"
lines—and medical care, the missionaries saved the government
a good deal of work and expense. And of course education
which made the natives more efficient in work for the whites,

* At the trial of Kenyatta, described below, in Chapter 9, it became necessary
for the prosecution to prove translations of one or two documents written in a
relatively uncommon African language by Paul Ngei, one of the defendants. The
prosecution, meticulous in the fulfilment of such requirements—in a fashion very
different from its readiness, which we shall see below, to pay high prices for perjured evidence—called as a witness an elderly Canadian lady who had worked
for over half a century as a missionary in the area where the language was spoken,
and of course knew it well. All that she had to do in her evidence, to start with, was
to produce translations of the documents into English and to say that they were
correct. Then, in cross-examination, I questioned her on lines prepared for me by
Ngei, saying: "Could not this or that particular passage mean so-and-so (more
helpful to Ngei's case than her translation)?" Three times her answer was: "Yes,
Mr. Pritt, looking at the words again, I think they could bear the meaning you
suggest." But the fourth time, she answered: "No, Mr. Pritt, I do not think so. If
the meaning you suggest had been intended, the words would have been . . ." and
she gave me a short sentence in the language. I replied that I of course accepted
what she said, but that I did not know the language, and she said: "Oh! No, but
I gave the words so that *Mr.* Ngei could follow." The use of the title *Mr.* to refer
to a native was so horrifying to the whites present, and above all to the magistrate,
that one could hear a gasp of horror. I do not think that the old lady was deliberately baiting the racialists; she was just using her own human and Christian
courtesy towards the natives to whom she had thought it right to devote her life.
   It is not surprising that in my final speech I suggested that the prosecution had
selected her as a witness in order to claim that not every witness it called was a
liar.

but did not go far enough to "give them ideas above their station", was valuable. In this respect, the needs of the rulers to have the masses educated corresponded exactly to those of the British ruling class around the middle of the nineteenth century.*

What the missionaries did for education, whilst as I have said it was much better than nothing, did not go very far. In the Kenyatta trial, one of the native witnesses for the prosecution, an intelligent girl who had attended a missionary school for three years and worked as a barmaid and a police spy, asserted —to explain why she had made a series of written statements to the police which were untrue and contradictory—that she was illiterate. When I suggested that after three years at school she must at least be able to read and write, every white in the Court laughed heartily, and the magistrate and the prosecution counsel assured me that that much schooling really could not carry her that far.

Another development of Kenyatta and his movement throws some light on the education available. In the early days after the Second World War, when Kenyatta was at liberty, he and his followers, asserting that both missionary and government education were alike inadequate and anti-native, started a "Kikuyu Independent Schools Association", to which the poor Africans contributed vast sums out of their scanty pence to build schools "independent" of the missionaries and government, so that their children could be "non-colonially" educated. Many such schools were built, and many children taught in them. Their value was demonstrated by the actions taken by the government after the "Emergency" was declared in 1952 with the object of destroying the mass party, the Kenya African Union, and Kenyatta himself. They closed all the "K.I.S.A." schools and took over the buildings, on the allegation that the schools were subversive. In a noble sense of the word, they of course were.

I must deal here with the position of natives engaged in

* When the British colonised the areas which were later called Kenya, and met with the familiar problem of deciding on one language in which the government and the natives could communicate, instead of having to use a dozen or more tribal languages, they did not select English, as was often done, for the reason that it would have enabled the more lively of the natives to read such books as those of Marx and Engels, but introduced Swahili, a language spoken in many coastal regions, but as much a foreign language in the interior as English was. Marx was not yet published in that language.

industries, to which I referred above. The story bears a broad similarity to similar developments in Britain at an earlier period, with in substance the same ruling class and the same predatory capitalists resisting every attempt to compel them to take safety measures and every effort of their workers to form trade unions. There were differences, of course; the colonial government was more reactionary than a home government would dare to be, and the only public opinion which might have affected it was in effect that constituted by the industrialists and like-minded whites. And the natives would be—at any rate at first and for a long time—"green" and largely defenceless against employers who could rely on the government to shoot demonstrators, and to justify the shootings in any subsequent enquiry. It is not surprising that in the early part of the twentieth century, when all sorts of industries were being launched on colonies by companies formed in London, prospectuses persuading investors to "risk" their money in colonial ventures used the phrase "labour cheap and docile" so often that it became a scornful slogan among the few anti-imperialists who came forward to protest.

I should deal here, rather than in the following chapter, with one particular aspect of the Courts in the colonies, which is both more significant and more important than might be expected, namely the staffing of these Courts, particularly for criminal cases. In most colonies, these are a very high proportion of all the cases, both because natives would seldom have enough property to lead to civil litigation and because so much of what the whites impose on the natives is enforced by criminal legislation and proceedings (one has only to mention the pass-laws of South Africa, which led to tens of thousands of prosecutions, and indeed those of colonial Kenya too). Superficially, one might expect a layman to say: "Staffing? What's the difficulty? Appoint judges to try the cases." But the system with which the colonists were already familar was one which did not, at home, empower a judge to try any major case by himself, but entrusted the decision of "guilty or not guilty" to a jury. Lawyers, and indeed governing organs generally, are conservative, and they would naturally think of a jury as something essential. In that case, as soon as they began to organise their Courts in the colonies, they would be confronted by two main problems. The first was simple and practical; could they find in the colony enough people who knew English to supply juries for the cases they expected to have to try? The sort of difficulty they met was illustrated by a case I conducted some years ago in the Privy Council on appeal from India, in which a number of men had been tried on a serious charge before a judge and a jury of five. (The traditional English number of twelve was often reduced in many colonies, to meet the difficulty of finding enough men to try the cases.) The trial had been conducted in English, and my clients had been convicted. They appealed in India, and by the time the appeal came on for hearing they had obtained pretty reliable information that at least two members of the jury understood very little English. They raised this as an additional ground of appeal—conclusive, of course if it stood—and supported it by an affidavit. The prosecution, more concerned to maintain the conviction than to ascertain the facts and see that real justice was done, submitted that the evidence in the affidavit was only hearsay. The Court upheld this objection, and the argument on the appeal went on. Before it came to an end, my clients succeeded in obtaining clear and direct evidence to the effect that at least two of the jurors knew substantially no English. They accordingly renewed their application to have this point argued. The prosecution, of the same mind as before, objected that a "new" point should not be allowed to be taken at such a late stage of the argument. The Court agreed, the hearing went on, and the convictions were affirmed. By this time the appellants had no money left, but they were able to arrange for the application to the Privy Council for special leave to appeal, and for the substantive appeal, if leave were granted, to be carried forward *in forma pauperis* (without fee), and I argued the case in the Privy Council. The presiding judge, Lord Atkin, and his colleagues grew pink with indignation, and allowed the appeal. They set the convictions aside. But they quite correctly ruled that such a "trial" did not amount to a trial at all, that my clients had therefore not been tried, and that they could still be prosecuted. The prosecuting authorities in India, still ready to do anything to get my clients convicted, prosecuted again, taking care that the jury should be composed of people who really knew English. My clients were then acquitted.

So much for the first of the two main problems which I mentioned as confronting colonial governments seeking to prosecute, and considering the question of the use of juries. The second was not so simple, and might well not be mentioned in public at all: could they rely on juries of which some members or indeed all members might be natives, to convict natives? And, if not, could they be brazen enough to provide juries of whites to try whites, whilst trying natives without juries, and if so in what classes of cases? And, if jurors were scarce or "unreliable", could they safely adopt the "assessor" system, under which a few laymen, generally three or five, sit with the judge and give at the end of the hearing their opinion on the guilt or innocence of the accused, whilst the judge often has the right to disagree with the assessors, or with some of them if they are not unanimous, and to give the verdict he himself favours.

In most colonies, and especially in British India, these problems received various solutions, not just from colony to colony, but within a colony or a province, according to the supply of potential jurymen or assessors and to their degree of "reliability". In a few areas, it was possible to maintain the jury system intact, with no more change than a reduction of the number required to sit on each case. In some, whites accused of murder or other grave crimes could insist on a white jury, whilst natives accused of similar offences might be tried by judge alone, or by judge and assessors. In other areas, assessors always sat, the judges being sometimes entitled to overrule them and sometimes not. And in yet other areas, trials were simply by judge alone. In one important province in British India, jury trial was universal *except* on charges of murder; one would normally think that juries were especially necessary for murder, but the British rulers had feared that they could not rely on natives to convict natives of murder in cases with any political flavour. As was inevitable, these various modes of trial existing side by side in various areas of one country led to a good deal of "jockeying" by prosecuting authorities, especially in political cases, to get cases tried in some district where the white judge would not be hampered by a jury or even by assessors. This happened in the notorious Meerut case, where many months and many tens of thousands of pounds were spent in prosecuting a group of British and Indian industrial workers for, in effect, trying to establish trade unions. And it happened very often in other cases, including that of Kenyatta, to which I will come in Chapter 9. The difficulty for "jockeys" is generally that it is a principle of good criminal procedure that trials should be held in the district where the crime is alleged to have been committed, and thus where witnesses are most likely to be available. This would have been, in Kenyatta's case, Nairobi, where or near where most of the evidence was to be found; but in Nairobi thousands of Africans would have attended the trial of their beloved leader and other popular figures, and it would have been under the eye of such public opinion as existed. So the government, almost as if it was determined that there should be no stage of the proceedings at which it was not violating elementary justice, entered into a sort of conspiracy to give it jurisdiction to try the case in a remote district which neither whites or natives were allowed to enter without special permission. The principle I mentioned was expressed in the Code applicable in Kenya in the usual terms that "every offence shall ordinarily be enquired into and tried by a Court within the local limits of whose jurisdiction it was committed". There were of course some qualifications to this rule, and one of them ran: "or within the local limits of whose jurisdiction the accused was apprehended". So the government, which had detained all the men concerned at the beginning of the Emergency declared some weeks before, on the basis that "their detention was necessary to the public safety", moved them up to the remote district I have mentioned, and there released them all from detention, thus impliedly asserting that their detention was no longer necessary to the public safety. Ten seconds later it apprehended them on a charge which implied that they were extremely dangerous, and thus created jurisdiction to try them in that area.

A case illustrative of the difficulties of the legislation covering the staffing of Courts, and therefore appropriate to be related here rather than in Chapter 9, came from what was then the Gold Coast some forty years ago. A doctor in the colonial medical service, stationed in Kumasi, the capital of Ashanti, was tried for murdering his wife, before a magistrate sitting alone, convicted, and sentenced to death; the case turned on slovenly legislation, applied in a slovenly fashion. The legislation provided that trials for murder in Ashanti should be held before juries unless this was impracticable; no investigation had been made into the practicability, and the trial had just gone ahead before the magistrate alone. I was asked to take the case before the Privy Council, once again *in forma pauperis*, and presented a good case for special leave to appeal, on the ground that the trial, held before a Court that had no jurisdiction to try it, was a nullity. I obtained leave without difficulty, for it is obviously a fundamental objection to any conviction that it was made by a Court which had no jurisdiction to try the case. When the substantive appeal came on, the judges realised that if I succeeded on this point, as I was very likely to do, the awkward scandal would arise that a good many natives had already been tried without juries, convicted of murder, and hanged. They therefore turned to examine whether the evidence as a whole was so utterly insufficient that, even under the narrow rules which they applied to hearing criminal appeals, the conviction must be set aside. They concluded that this was the position, that the question of jurisdiction need not therefore be decided, and that my client must be acquitted. (It was just one of the ironies of litigation that, if that had been the sole ground on which I had sought to obtain leave to appeal, I should probably not have succeeded.)*

So much for the background of the colonial systems in which the lawyers have to play their parts. I have now to discuss their role in the colonies. But before I do so I must examine the arguments or excuses put forward by the defenders of the colonial system, and test them by the light of reality. Apart from the general chatter about our "trusteeship" for the natives, and about their inborn and incurable "inferiority"— "they are just children, you know"—(as if children don't grow up), more precise and positive claims for the virtues of the colonising powers are often put forward. We are told that they have built railways and roads for the natives, provided them with work, and have given them a higher standard of living. When we ask, "higher than what?" it is sometimes claimed that

---

* Barristers are sometimes thanked by their clients for winning their cases for them, but not always. This particular client, saved from the gallows and secured many months of back pay and a pension, by the labour of two substantial arguments before the Privy Council, with all the preparatory work involved, did not even send me a postcard of thanks.

it is higher than it was before, and sometimes that it is higher than it would have been if we had never colonised them at all.

Let me examine these claims. That we have provided railways and roads is true, as a bare fact; but for whom did we in truth provide them? The answer is that we provided them just where and in so far as we needed them for our own governmental or industrial purposes. Roads may have seemed at first sight a great benefit in many areas where there were only narrow tracks before; but the latter were in general sufficient for native needs, since they had little wheeled traffic. Good highways were in fact emphatically for *our* advantage.*

On the alleged higher standing of living, one has to begin with the fact that, before they were colonised, the peoples lived their own lives and did not in general starve, and that, under colonial rule, with the benefit of a capitalist economy, when the whole structure of their lives had been torn up in the interests of the whites, they were very often more than half starved. In terms of money, which had meant little or nothing to them before, it might be claimed that a family would now often have 30s. or so a month, when before it had had no money but lived and was housed in its own village, and had enough to eat. It could easily appear that those who left their villages to work in industries were "richer". But there was no advantage in giving up one's own way of life in exchange for a precarious industrial position, with all the risks of dismissal and of unemployment at the bottom end of the scale of another world's way of life.

On education, the natives would gradually gain a little in terms of general education on European lines, the inadequacy of which I have already described, and at the price of having to master a foreign language, English, Swahili, or something else.

It would be travelling too far from my topic to consider the position of newly independent ex-colonies, under neo-colonialism and capitalist "aid to underdeveloped countries", and I can now turn to the direct task of examining the role of lawyers under the colonial system.

* I recall that in one part of Kenya, where I often had to travel long distances on important but extremely bad roads, I asked why the roads were not made better, since the whites had to use them constantly. I was met with the answer that a great deal of European money had been invested in railways covering the same routes, and that if the roads were improved the railways would lose traffic and be unable to pay the interest on their building loans. After independence, the by no means rich independent Kenya improved these roads.

8

The Role of Lawyers in Colonies

Here I have to examine, against the background of the colonialist domination of colonial peoples, the law applied to the
colonies, legislation therein, the actual structure and staffing
of the legal machine, including the judges, and lawyers practising privately.

The situation existing before the arrival of British colonists in
the various British colonies varied from colony to colony.
Many colonies were "settlements" of whites in sparsely inhabited territories or territories inhabited only by people with
little in the way of government machinery corresponding to
European ideas. Others were already colonised territories taken
by force of arms from other colonialist powers (like Guyana and
some islands in the West Indies, and Ceylon). Others again
were captured by force of arms from peoples and governments
already pretty fully developed (like India, Burma, and Quebec).
When it came to determining the basic legal situation in the
various territories, the three classes I have mentioned were
differently treated.

In the first and most numerous class, which included most
African colonies but many others, the habits and outlooks of
natives received little consideration, and the colony was treated
in accordance with one or other of two recognised principles,
the first applying to such territories acquired by conquest and
the second to those acquired by settlement. In the case of
conquest, the view was that, as conqueror, the colonising power
was an absolute despot, entitled to deal with the territory and
its inhabitants as it wished, and to impose on them any laws it
chose.

This was illustrated by the very first political case in which
I was engaged, *Rex* v. *Earl of Crewe, ex parte Sekgome*, reported in
the Law Reports (1910) 2 K.B. 576. Lord Crewe was the

Secretary of State for the Colonies, and Sekgome was an African chief in the (then) Bechuanaland Protectorate. He had in some way displeased the British authorities, and they had put him in prison, without charge or trial, on the basis of a Proclamation which they had issued, empowering themselves to do so. (Outside India, such behaviour was not then as fashionable as it became later, and there was no general legislation authorising it.)

Sekgome sought to test the legality of this proceeding. It would have been useless to try to do so in Bechuanaland, so he thought of testing it in the British Courts, either by applying for Habeas Corpus, or by an action for false imprisonment. The difficulty was that those who were actually detaining Sekgome were in Bechuanaland and not in Britain, and that no one in Britain had power to release him, which would make them liable to Habeas Corpus, or to an action for false imprisonment, if they failed to do so. But the British High Commissioner for South Africa, Lord Selborne, under whose control Bechuanaland stood, might be sued if he were at home in England on leave. This happened to be the case at the time, so a writ was prepared and given to a writ-server to serve on him, as he was just about to leave England. After some amusing manœuvres, in which he displayed all the ingenuity of the habitual writ-dodging debtor, he managed to get away without being served; so Sekgome's advisers had to think again. As a result of their thought they brought Habeas Corpus proceedings against the Secretary of State for the Colonies, against whom it could be argued that, having power to order the release of Sekgome, he was responsible for his detention, and could have a Habeas Corpus order made against him.

The case was argued in two Courts, the High Court and the Court of Appeal. There were two issues, the first, a technical one, was whether Habeas Corpus proceedings would lie against the Minister, and the second, the one of substance and importance, was that of the validity of the detention under the Proclamation. Having been brought up to believe that the British government ruled its colonial territories for the benefit of the natives, and treated them all fairly, in the spirit of civil liberty, I was naïve enough to be surprised that the then Liberal government should take the technical point as well as the other (it would not surprise me now!). In the end, the Courts held the detention was valid, and the Proclamation lawful; the technical point was not decided.

In the case of territories not conquered but settled, the incomers were held in law to have carried with them the law of England, and to be both entitled to the protection of that law and bound to obey it.

In Quebec and some other territories with well-established legal systems, such as the "Custom of Paris" which the French government had applied in Quebec—and on which later the Code Napoléon and the Code Civil de Québec were based—it was usual, but not automatic or compulsory, for the British to retain the legal system as it stood, subject to amendment, of course. Such amendment could be introduced by, for example, the legislature they established in "Lower Canada", as Quebec was named, and later in the Dominion of Canada, set up in 1867. In Ceylon, South Africa, and Guyana, much the same course was followed, resulting at times in odd mixtures of Roman-Dutch and English law, both interesting and profitable to lawyers. In India, where the many provinces and Princes' States had various well-established systems of law, often not readily understood by English lawyers, English law was introduced in most fields of law, but the elaborate family and succession laws of both Hindus and Moslems were in general left intact.

In territories where for one reason or another the incomers thought it useful or necessary to "start from scratch" by setting up a system of law for the territory, this was normally done by legislation, at first in the form I have already mentioned of Orders in Council, and then by one form or another of local legislation. This legislation, which had to be applied and understood by all sorts of people, including many whose mother tongue was not English, had to be couched in written form in pretty close detail. But for what one might call practical everyday legislation—for example, such things as the law of contract and tort, not immediately and directly related to the maintenance of colonialist power and to the class struggle—the problem was often dealt with shortly and comprehensively by enacting that the law of England as it stood at some date, perhaps the date of the establishment of the colony, should apply. Sometimes, in rather slovenly fashion, it was provided that the law of England should apply "as far as it was applicable to the conditions of the colony", a provision which led to endless litigation which might well have been avoided by clearer legislation. (I once had a case which came from Singapore to the Privy Council to decide whether the English legislation on rent restriction applied in that colony.)

There were instances, too, where it was merely laid down that any matter not covered expressly by the law applying in the Colony should be dealt with in accordance with the dictates of "equity and good conscience", which led a Court in the Sudan, staffed by English colonial judges, to apply the Sale of Goods Act of Great Britain.

Much must depend, of course, on the quality of legal personnel available for the work of legislation and of administration in the colonies. In developed countries, like Quebec and India, there was relatively little difficulty. In Quebec, there were lawyers trained in the Roman-law-based jurisprudence of France who were well equal to the not too difficult task of running the country on French lines under British government. In India, many well-qualified English lawyers were drawn in, including judges of the High Courts recruited from among trained English lawyers, and there were very many educated Indians for important lesser (including judicial) posts. (The Indians, quick and nimble in thought, and very ingenious, are "natural" lawyers, and naturally litigious too. I could never understand why there were so many "lawyers' touts" working to beat up litigation, for I thought that everyone who could possibly afford to litigate was already doing so, without any such encouragement!) And in settled colonies with largely white populations, like Australia, and most of "English" Canada, lawyers were available in reasonable numbers.

In the typical "undeveloped" colony with a non-white population, of which there were so many, each with its separate administration, the provision of even government legal personnel created a great problem. It was not merely difficult to recruit lawyers with the right "colonialist" attitude, but to recruit them at all in anything like sufficient numbers. In every colony, the Governor had to have a legal adviser—generally the Attorney-General (to whom and to whose duties I must return in a moment)—a Supreme Court with at least one and more often several judges, a large number of magistrates, and government prosecutors in some numbers, all of whom would have to come from Britain, or occasionally from Australia or New Zealand. And, in one way or another, there would have to be found some few private legal practitioners, not only for civil litigation, but also to defend some at any rate of the many natives charged with serious offences. (These practitioners might or might not be drawn from England, depending on the conditions and the population.)

I will deal first with government legal personnel, required for the various functions I have stated, and capable of helping a strong executive to hold down the population in time of trouble, and of serving the manifold operations of industry and agriculture as well as of administration itself, all at not too great expense. How were they to work, and how were they to be recruited? I must start with the structure "on the ground" and then look at the recruiting. The structure, of which I have already written a little, was fairly simple. I need write no more about the judges and magistrates; but must deal further with the Attorney-General. He not only advised the Governor on all questions of law; he sat in the Legislative Council, if there was one, and certainly in the Governor's Council; he was the head of the whole Public Prosecutor's Department; and in all cases of any importance he would appear in Court for the government. He would also have to draft all the legislation of the colony, a formidable task calling for considerable knowledge and ability, even if in many fields of legislation he would have the help of model legislation prepared in the Colonial Office in London for adaptation and application in each colony. And when drafting legislation, he had the extra responsibility that what he drafted would tend to become law without modification, for there would be little or none of the detailed criticism of draft legislation which is available in Britain not only in Parliament when the draft legislation comes before it but also by public opinion.

When one considers the recruiting of this vast array of trained lawyers, mostly from Britain, one must wonder how enough staff of even moderate quality was ever found. Some of it came from Ireland and Scotland, countries of good education and inadequate home demand for professional workers, and a little from Australia and New Zealand, but the greatest proportion, by far, came from the English Bar. Colonial lawyers were made available by the curious structure of the profession in England in which, at any rate up to the Second World War, those who became barristers were in a sense engaging in a gamble. They were almost certain to earn next to nothing for their first few years, and then they would either slowly realise that they were not going to succeed at the Bar but must try to get one of the many employments which the qualifications of a barrister plus a little experience would help them to get, or would find that they were going to succeed at the Bar, and could go on to do so. The semi-failures, often people of considerable ability but by no means always so, provided a rich recruiting ground for the colonial legal service, which could offer them at least a secure living from the moment of appointment, plus prospects of promotion to a certain number of attractive and well-paid posts, such as Chief Justiceships, and pensioned retirement at a fairly early age. Apart from India, which recruited a fair number of lawyers from among those who had already succeeded pretty well in England, the great majority of colonies were staffed by the "drop-outs" of the English Bar, plus a few solicitors.

The result was that the colonial legal service was in the main staffed by "the second eleven". They were at the best fairly competent, but they embarked on their careers with all the outlooks and prejudices required for the colonies—or in the rare cases where they were not so equipped they soon took on the necessary colour (or left the service). They of course started on the lower rungs of the ladder, and expected to move up slowly so long as they did not displease their superiors. The lowest rung was normally that of magistrate, and thus these relatively young and "green" orthodox products of middle- or upper middle-class homes, often that type of conservative which calls itself non-political, would work in a strange country, with a strange and sometimes a bad climate, and little access to law books or to the advice or help of less inexperienced colleagues, and would hear charges, often very serious ones, levelled against "natives" whose way of life was wholly strange to them, and would arrive as best they could at conclusions as to which

witness was to be believed, and as to what if any offence was
established by the evidence. Typically, they would soon be
equipped with every imaginable anti-native prejudice. If
they were in a region of Kenya inhabited by Kikuyus, for example, they would have it drummed into their ears from the
moment of their arrival in the colony that "all Kikuyus are
liars", an axiom acted on by the government lawyers unless
and until they called them as prosecution witnesses.

Like their stipendiary colleagues in England—see Chapter 8
of Book 2—they would normally accept police evidence. Among
the difficulties besetting them would be the appalling obstacles
of interpretation. The Court language would be English or
occasionally some such language as Swahili. The witnesses and
the accused in most cases would speak a local language, often a
well-developed and highly elaborate one, and interpreters of
varying degrees of competence and honesty would have to
interpret. It would be quite common for double translation to
be involved, for there would be no interpreter available who
knew both the native tongue and English. Thus questions which
might not be simple, and the answers to which might lead to
sentences of death or of long imprisonment, would start in
English, go into the intermediate language with inevitably some
change of meaning, and on into the local language with similar
changes. The answer by the accused or the witness to the
question as it reached him would then start on a similarly
complicated return journey, and would appear on the face of
the record as the answer of the deponent to the question
originally put. This grave obstacle to proper understanding can
be illustrated by the experience of a friend of mine, a man of
great ability who ultimately rose to the highest post in the
colonial legal service. He started his career as a magistrate,
and had to try a not very simple charge of attempted rape.
He listened carefully to all the evidence of the prosecution—
of course, through interpretation—and then, as a good and
conscientious lawyer, came to a conclusion which he put to the
interpreter thus:

"Tell the accused that I am now ruling that the evidence
does not disclose a *prima facie* case of attempted rape, but
does disclose a *prima facie* case of indecent assault."

The language in which the interpreter and the accused were communicating with one another happened to be a primitive "pidgin English", and my friend was astonished to hear his careful ruling transmitted to the accused in the following form:

"Beak say, you no. . . . 'em plenty, you only. . . . 'em small."

I can give two illustrations from my own experience of the limited competence and understanding which some of these colonial lawyers display. They both happen to concern Attorneys-General, which makes the cases the more lamentable because men are not normally promoted to such posts until they have had a good deal of experience, and because Attorneys-General, even from small colonies, are generally entitled, on promotion, to higher posts in the judiciary than other lawyers.

The first of these cases was that of an Indian Tamil clerk in Malaya, who was attacked and very nearly killed, and left lying near to death under the tropical sun for many hours before he was discovered and taken to hospital, where he lay unconscious for some days.

He ultimately recovered, and a prosecution was then launched not against the persons who had nearly murdered him, but against him himself, the charge being that, when he was found, he had in his "possession"—although unconscious—a revolver, an offence punishable in Malaya at that period by death, without any alternative. On his trial, the assessors voted for his acquittal, but the European judge, being entitled to ignore their view, convicted him and sentenced him to death. The trial had, however, been so badly conducted in various ways that an appellate Court ordered a new trial; and on that new trial the prosecution embarked on a piece of rascality unusual even in the worst and most unscrupulous of criminal prosecutions. A police officer who had not even been called as a witness at the first trial went into the witness-box and swore that, a few hours after the man had been taken to hospital, and when according to the medical evidence he was completely unconscious and not expected to survive, he went into the hospital, interviewed the man, and obtained from him a complete confession of his crime. He explained the absence of any document by saying that the confession was made orally. This plainly false evidence, unaided even by any explanation as to why it had not been brought forward at the first trial, was rejected by the assessors at this second trial, but it was accepted by the judge, and the man was once again convicted and sentenced to death.

At this stage the government of India, hearing how its Tamil citizen was being treated, asked me to act for him by taking the case to the Privy Council. I gladly took it up, and of course had no difficulty in obtaining special leave to appeal. When the substantive appeal came on for hearing, I was in the middle of another case, a long one, in the Privy Council, which I could not leave; so I had to hand the case back, and it was conducted, of course successfully, by another barrister. At this stage I reach the illustration of the degree of understanding that the particular Attorney-General involved was capable of showing. He was sent over by the government of Malaya to take part in the argument before the Privy Council; and, as the counsel appearing in the various cases there normally all lunched at that time in the same dining-room, I found myself at a table next to this Attorney-General, who—although he did not realise it—could not possibly win his case. I heard him announce in a loud and lordly voice, and with apparent pleasure: "Yes, the appeal will be dismissed tomorrow, I shall cable out at once, and the fellow will be hanged on the following morning."

The other illustration is not very different; it was the "Case of the Chinese cook", an interesting case which I described fully in Chapter 11 of the third volume of my *Autobiography*. I need not give the details of this fascinating and complicated case, but will content myself with the observation that I have never known a case in which there were so many reasons why an appeal by my client was bound to succeed. The appeal, which came from Aden, went not to the Privy Council but to the Court of Appeal for Eastern Africa, which sat at Nairobi, and I went out there to conduct it. One of the practical difficulties of barristers is to know just when their cases are likely to come on for hearing, for Courts generally put several cases in the list for hearing each day, and each case starts as soon as the one in front of it ends. No one can be sure when a case will end, so every barrister concerned in any case in the List will ask all those who are in front of him: "How long will your case last?" The answer depends not only on how long the appellant's counsel will take, but upon the question whether he will make sufficient impression on the Court to lead it to call on the other side to argue, and the further question, how long that side takes. So, in this case, when the counsel in the next case asked me, I replied that I would take about a day, that my opponent would certainly be called on, and that I would not be called on to reply. All this duly worked out as I said; but I happened to hear the counsel ask my opponent for his estimate—always a prudent thing to do—and was astonished to hear him say: "Pritt has no earthly chance of making out a case, so I shall not be called on, and your case should start as soon as Pritt sits down." I would not have thought that anyone could have been so utterly ignorant of a case which he was presumably ready to conduct.

Whilst the law which all these legal officials, including the judges, had to administer, and the procedure in both criminal and civil cases, were of English origin and structure, there were necessarily a good many differences apart from that of quality. They derived partly from the judges having had little or no experience of practising as barristers, and partly from the paucity of first-class advocates in private practice appearing before them. As I mentioned in Chapter 7 of Book 2, much of the good quality of Court work in England is due to the judges having practised for a number of years as barristers and thus being able to understand the habits and the problems of barristers, and from the latter knowing this. As a result, the two groups of lawyers can argue cases, and hear arguments, with a full understanding of each other and with reasonable courtesy. (I have learnt by experience that in at any rate most of the countries where the judges are civil servants, appointed and trained as judges from the start of their careers, and have never conducted cases, the relations between the judges and the advocates are often hostile, and there is no real understanding or co-operation.) As a general rule, the judges in the colonial Courts will have had no experience of practice at the Bar, except perhaps in their earlier years in England before they joined the colonial service; they will, it is true, in many instances have conducted prosecutions in one colony or another, but that is substantially different from the ordinary work of a barrister.

The judges, too, will have all sorts of minor but not unimportant difficulties to contend with, such as the inadequate supply of law-books which are essential to the argument of any point of law in a country where case-law applies. In theory, every colony is properly equipped in this respect, but in practice this does not work out very well. Books will of course only be readily available in the capital city, or in one or two other cities in large colonies, and there will not often be many copies of any one book. At one stage of the appeals in the long Kenyatta trials a number of points of law had to be argued before two judges of the Supreme Court, sitting at Kitale some 250 miles from Nairobi. I warned them that I would have to cite a number of Law Reports, and they said that that presented no difficulty, as the books could be brought from Nairobi. But when we got down to the arguments—where in England each judge and each advocate would have a copy of each book before him, and could thus easily follow the argument as the counsel arguing read out from his copy of the book—it turned out that there was only one copy of each book. The judges and the opposing counsel had to listen as best they could while I read what I needed to read, and then I handed the book up to the judges to read, and waited while they did so. My opponent was able to look over my shoulder as I read, and might be able to borrow the book on perhaps the following day if the judges were not keeping it for themselves. (And all this was repeated perhaps twenty times for twenty citations.)

There are further differences and difficulties arising from the often mediocre quality of the advocates in private practice. In England, where barristers are able to present their clients' cases with competence, and often with courage, their work is often very helpful to the judges, enabling them to give better judgments. In colonies, whilst the position varies greatly from one territory to another, it is generally much less satisfactory. Sometimes there are very few advocates; sometimes, where whites are available, they tend to be men of poor quality, who would not have come to the colony at all if they had been able to get work in England; in any case they have little understanding of, or sympathy for, the outlook of their native clients. If Indian advocates are available—as is often the case, for example, in East Africa—the position will be better, owing to the skill and ingenuity, and often the courage, of Indians who, as I mentioned above, make good lawyers. African advocates of good quality are seldom to be found except on the West Coast of Africa and in the West Indies, owing to the practical difficulties for Africans to get educated and admitted. But the position here too is improving.

Perhaps the greatest of all the difficulties and defects of the advocates in private practice—which as I have said means mostly practice in criminal cases—is the difficulty of their standing up and fighting for their clients on equal terms against the public prosecutors or "Crown Counsel" who conduct the prosecutions. These latter, even if they may not be very competent, have many advantages. They are part of the white ruling-class establishment. They are on friendly terms with the white judges and magistrates, who belong to the same colonial legal service as they do, and they grow confidently accustomed to having these judges and magistrates accepting their arguments and the evidence of their witnesses. They will often bully the advocates who appear for the accused, and the latter, unless they are resourceful Indians or natives of some prestige and experience, will not always have the toughness and the courage to stand up to the Crown Counsel, as they must fear to lose their cases—and thus in the long run their practice—if they fight really hard and incur the displeasure of the judges and magistrates.

These judges and magistrates are, as I have already mentioned, subject to no influence from public opinion, save what is in reality that of themselves and their own circle. There were many moments in the various cases I conducted in various colonies, above all Kenya, when I was putting before the Courts arguments which objectively speaking were unanswerable and should compel the Court to rule in my favour on important points, and in favour of my native clients and against the government, when I was suddenly checked in my optimism by realising that, if the judge or the magistrate were to rule, as he should, in my favour, he would not merely lose all hope of being promoted to higher judicial office but would be immediately subjected to intolerable social boycott. (And yet, now and then, I found a magistrate taking courage to rule correctly.)

9

Some Illustrative Cases

In this chapter, a sort of parallel to Chapter 4, I give a number of examples of typical and significant cases heard in the colonies.

The first is that of Julius Nyereri, tried in the middle of 1958 in what was at the time the mandated territory of Tanganyika. I went out to Dar-es-Salaam to defend him on a charge of criminal libel. He was and is a man of statesman-like qualities, gentle, firm, and shrewd; and to prosecute him on such a charge at that time, even if the prosecution had been properly prepared and conducted, was an act of short-sighted folly. He was the President of the Tanganyika African National Union (T.A.N.U.), and probably the most generally and deeply beloved leader anywhere in East Africa. Within less than three years he was to become the Chief Minister of Tanganyika, soon after the Prime Minister of independent Tanganyika, and only a little later the President. I asserted in Court at the time that the prosecution had hastened Tanganyikan independence by five years.

The case was a curious one, with a sudden element of drama in the middle of it. T.A.N.U., a mass organisation of great efficiency, used to issue periodically a cyclostyled newssheet called *Sauti ya Tanu* ("Voice of Tanu"), with a circulation of about 200. Nyereri, who had received many reports of bad administration in various districts of the territory, and had learnt that complaints made privately to the government or its officers not only produced no remedy but sometimes had un-fortunate results for those who ventured to make them, decided that the time had come to make some of them public; and he did so in *Sauti ya Tanu* of the 27th May, 1958. His statements would never have led to prosecution in England, although they might possibly have helped to procure a remedy. But the

Tanganyika government, some six weeks later, prosecuted him for criminally libelling two District Commissioners who could fairly be recognised as the objects of his criticisms in the article. I will call them A and B. It came out at the trial that in all those six weeks the government had not asked either A or B for his version of the incidents in which he was alleged to be at fault. It was thus exposed as ready to prosecute the beloved leader of the people for whom it was "trustee" under the United Nations, without even knowing or trying to find out whether what he wrote was true (and therefore not criminal), and as ready, when faced with serious complaints put forward about its servants by the most important and responsible African in the territory, not only to prosecute but also to fail to enquire whether there was anything which it ought to remedy.

The prosecution's first major misbehaviour—or, it may be, blunder—in the hearing was that it did not call either A or B to give evidence, thus leaving it open to the defence to call witness after witness to prove this, that or the other misconduct on their part without their having the opportunity to answer, deny or explain. The prosecution asserted that it was following a proper course in this, claiming that it was for the defence to prove what it could, and that A and B could then be called to give evidence "in rebuttal", after the defence had closed its case. But rebuttal evidence can be given in criminal cases only by leave, and leave is not readily given. The real motive for holding back A and B may well have been the desire to save these "sacrosanct" officers from a damaging cross-examination by me, which might have gone a long way towards establishing the defence, the strength of which must have been unknown to the government, as it had not asked A and B for their versions.

Anyway, the prosecution closed its case without calling the two men, and I and Nyereri himself, and my colleagues in the defence, wishing for good political reasons to show our determination to fight the case on the merits, decided not to argue, as we might well have done, that the case should be dismissed because the prosecution had not made out any case for us to answer, but to go straight ahead with my opening speech and the evidence, starting naturally with Nyereri as the first witness. What we had to prove to establish a defence was that what he had written was true and was published in the public interest. To prove the facts, which were known to Nyereri himself only by reliable reports, i.e., by hearsay, it was necessary to call witnesses, one of whom was a well-known chief (of the sort I have discussed in Chapter 6). The evidence of Nyereri went off quietly enough, and we then called the chief I have mentioned. We were not expecting anything in the nature of a crisis, but the really wicked behaviour of the government soon brought one. The chief in question, whose alleged unfair treatment by A was criticised in *Sauti ya Tanu*, had been a chief for 32 years. He knew that if he gave evidence he would incur the extreme disapproval of the government which had appointed him and kept him in office for a generation, but could dismiss him summarily at any time; but he felt under a duty to give evidence and was ready to go into the witness-box, as were several other African witnesses. What the government did was, on the very day he was giving evidence—and he was almost certain to be giving evidence also on the following day—to serve upon him an Order deposing him as Chief "in the interests of peace, order, and good government", and exiling him to another part of the extensive territory of Tanganyika. The order stated that he had been guilty of carrying on "a corrupt and despotic regime", and that this had been proved by "the sworn testimony of numerous witnesses" (all of them, if they existed at all, having been examined behind his back and without notice to him, after enquiry, presumably in the very area in which they were simultaneously failing to enquire into the misconduct alleged against A).

The Order had been made by the "Officer administering the government"—the highest official there, as there was at the moment no Governor—and was on that very day handed to the press for publication. And, as if they were determined to make their behaviour as scandalous as it could possibly be, a "government spokesman" let himself go to the press in further abuse of the Chief. One was left wondering, apart from the effect of this behaviour on the hearing of the case, what sort of a government there could be which could have continued to employ for 32 years such a blackguard as they were alleging the Chief to be.

It is impossible to attribute even to that government ignorance of the rule of English law that it is a most serious contempt of Court to intimidate or to attack in any way witnesses who are giving or are about to give evidence in a criminal case, and they must simply have been behaving as if they were above the law. In a sense they were, but they were below the future which awaited them—the independence of Tanganyika.

When we came into Court the next morning, with the news of what had been done known to everyone, I submitted to the magistrate that the "Officer administering the government", the "government spokesman", and the *Tanganyika Standard* which had published their statements, ought to be made the object of immediate proceedings for contempt of Court. The magistrate went so far as to direct that the officer who actually served the Order on the Chief and the editor of the newspaper— the two offenders least to be blamed—should appear before him. He said nothing about the two more serious offenders, or about putting the matter before the High Court, the only Court having power to deal with the contempt.

I told the magistrate that I and my colleagues would have to consider what ought to be done in the interests both of justice and of Nyereri himself, now that the government had openly intimidated not only the witness actually giving evidence— the Chief—but every other African witness we were going to call, all of whom would go into the witness-box with the knowledge that the Chief had hardly reached the witness- box before he was deposed, exiled and publicly abused. If a Chief could be dealt with in this way, what might happen to "ordinary" natives like themselves?

The case was then adjourned until the next day, and one can imagine that both the legal and the administrative members of the government, even if they were capable of what they had already done, must have had some anxious discussions in the meanwhile. One result, which even English lawyers who had learnt how far a ruling class will go when it wants to "keep people in their place" may find it hard to believe, was that in the end no one was punished for contempt of Court, and that the prosecution of Nyereri was allowed to continue, although in a truncated form.

On the following morning, the Attorney-General attended the Court—he had not been conducting the prosecution—made a long statement which if anything made the contempt of

Court a little worse, said nothing about anyone being prosecuted for it, and announced that one count in the charge against Nyereri, which concerned A, would be dropped, another which concerned only B would be maintained, and that a third which concerned them both would be amended by omitting all reference to A. I answered that if the contempt of Court were not brought before the High Court at once we would consider at our leisure whether we should bring it up ourselves, but that the urgent question was, what should be done with the case against Nyereri. On that, I said, no one would think that justice was being done if the case went on, that it was hopeless to expect any witnesses to go into the witness-box with any confidence, and that the whole case should be dropped at once, or dismissed by the magistrate. The magistrate ruled that the case must proceed in its truncated form, and adjourned it to the next day. He said that he himself would take no steps about the contempt.

I and my colleagues and Nyereri thought over the whole matter, and concluded that it would be hopeless to call any further witnesses at the price of their being victimised by the government; and on the resumed hearing we told the magistrate so. The Solicitor-General, who was conducting the prosecution, asked for leave to call rebutting evidence (in answer to Nyereri's evidence), which the magistrate refused. We said nothing more about going to the High Court for proceeding about contempt of Court, thinking it better to let sleeping dogs, or rather hyenas, lie.

The magistrate reserved his judgment for a few weeks, and then fined Nyereri £150 for half of what he had written, which no one would have ever dreamed of prosecuting in England. That was the end of the case in one sense, but one must surely count as part of its effects the independence of Tanganyika, which came within three-and-a-half years.

I move now to a case in India, which took place in the later years of the Second World War, i.e., before independence, for an account of the amazing misbehaviour of a Chief Justice, and of the natural but rather unworthy attempt of the Privy Council to help him out of the mess he had created. My client in this case, Devadhas Gandhi, son of Mahatma Gandhi, was the editor of an important English-language paper, *The*

Hindustan Times. He was prosecuted for contempt of Court under curious circumstances; the mere prosecution was bad enough in itself, but the way in which it was carried on made the matter far more serious.

In 1942 and 1943, there was a strong drive among European officials and "loyal" Indians (i.e., those loyal to British rule) to collect money from the public for various war purposes, and it was officially decided to put pressure on lawyers to subscribe. The whole "drive" was naturally opposed by many Indians who resented being asked to subscribe money to the "war effort" of a war into which their country had been taken without even a pretence of consultation. The pressure on lawyers to subscribe was operated through the Chief Justices of the various High Courts; and the Chief Justice involved in this case sent a circular letter to all his sessions judges (judges subordinate to him, who tried all serious criminal cases) directing them to take collections from the lawyers practising in their districts. This was crude enough, but one sessions judge made it cruder still by taking a collection in open Court from the lawyers engaged in a long murder trial, in which several of the accused were separately defended by different lawyers. By the time he came to take this collection it was fairly clear that two or three of the accused would be acquitted, and that one or two would probably be convicted; and on the last day of the trial the sessions judge invited the lawyers engaged in the case to subscribe to the Chief Justice's collection, and to lay their subscriptions on the table of the Court Clerk then and there, in the presence of the public. This the lawyers, with their hopes and fears about the fates of their clients, duly did, laying down substantial sums before the judge who held their clients' lives in his hands and was shortly to give judgment in which he was expected to free some of them and to send the others to the gallows.

The Hindustan Times commented on this in much the same fashion as a serious British paper would have done. Its criticism covered not only the sessions judge but also the Chief Justice, whose letter had started the train of events. For this, the journalist who had actually written the comment and Devadhas Gandhi, who as editor was responsible for publishing it, were prosecuted for contempt of Court. This prosecution, if properly conducted, would not have been an outstanding scandal, although it ought to have failed; but it was conducted most improperly. Contempt of Court is a matter with which Courts can properly deal of their own motion; and this Chief Justice proceeded to deal with this alleged instance of the offence in an odd fashion. The alleged contempt, it will be noticed, was not committed in Court, and was not an attack on the High Court or on the administration of justice, but was aimed at the sessions judge and the Chief Justice alone, in respect of conduct in what was in no sense part of their judicial work. Plainly, the Chief Justice should have let the prosecution, if one were brought at all, come before one of the other judges of the High Court, and he should have taken no part in it himself. But he did the exact opposite; he played all the roles in the prosecution and adjudication—in a sense, he even took part in the defence, to the latter's detriment. He initiated the proceedings; he directed that they should be heard before himself; he did much of the work that would ordinarily be done by a solicitor in England or a government advocate in India, namely, interviewing potential witnesses, taking statements from them, and deciding whether they should be called or not. When the case came on he called and examined the witnesses himself; and —perhaps the worst irregularity—he directed that a question of fact as to which there was an acute conflict, and on which a great deal depended, should not be decided on evidence but should be taken from the outset as concluded in a way which he laid down. (He thus succeeded in making himself a witness —and an uncontradictable witness—the victim, the solicitor, the prosecuting counsel, and the judge.)

He heard the evidence for the defence, so far as he had not excluded it by his advance determination of fact mentioned above, and then proceeded to give judgment in favour—in a sense—of himself, sentencing the writer of the article to a term of imprisonment, and the editor to a fine, with the usual alternative of imprisonment. The editor was not going to allow his employee to go to prison whilst he himself merely paid a fine; so he refused to pay, and went to prison. Both the convicted men asked the Chief Justice for a stay of execution pending a petition to the Privy Council for leave to appeal. This should certainly have been granted, but the Chief Justice refused it.

They petitioned the Privy Council for leave to appeal, employing me to appear for them. I obtained leave, and I won their appeal when it came on; they had served their sentences long before this happened. But the behaviour of the Privy Council was almost as odd, although in no sense so scandalous, as that of the Chief Justice. The facts of this case were so plainly outrageous that I expected to get leave to appeal in a quarter of an hour or twenty minutes; but I met with an unexpected and subborn resistance from the judges, due surely to a desire to save the Chief Justice's face. It was only after nearly three hours of hard fighting, almost as it were with bare fists, that I finally got leave.

In due course, the appeal itself came on for argument, and I waited with interest to see how the judges would deal with it, and whether they would try to find an escape route for the Chief Justice. The presiding judge was Lord Atkin, some of whose virtues I have already mentioned in Chapter 4. He had an ingenious mind, and was no doubt happy to get the matter disposed of, if he legitimately could, without too much advertisement of the conduct of the Chief Justice. I had not spent more than ten minutes "opening" the appeal when he said to me: "Mr. Pritt, has it occurred to you that the real position in this case may be that the article did not amount to a contempt of Court at all?" I had in fact thought of that possibility, but had not ventured to put it forward in the printed submissions which are always prepared in Privy Council appeals, so I made some gentle and welcoming answer. Lord Atkin then asked my opponent what his attitude was. The latter saw very quickly how he might get his client out without too much loss of face, and he knew that he could not hope to win the case; so he replied that if the Court was inclined to think the article was not a contempt he would find it difficult to argue that it was. That was the end of the appeal; it had lasted about 17 minutes.

I come now to the Kenyatta cases, which began in November 1952, and did not really finish until 1959. I have already written a good deal about them above. They form a very long story, which I will describe as briefly as possible—just sufficiently to show the class-warlike and unscrupulous behaviour of most of those acting for the government.

Kenyatta was President of the Kenya African Union

(K.A.U.), the one lawful political organisation of Africans in Kenya, with a large paid-up membership—at least 100,000. He was a greatly-loved leader, a shrewd politician, and— I was told—a speaker of great magnetism and power. (I say "I am told", for in all the years I knew him until just before Kenya became independent he had never been at liberty.)

Of his five co-accused, Kubai was a trade union leader of influence and prestige, friendly intelligent and resolute; Achieng Oneko was lively and witty, with a penetrating mind; Kaggia was a pleasant man, a deeply religious Christian; Ngei was a lively person, who did not come into the picture very strongly, as the charges against him were trivial and largely unconnected with the cases of the others. Karumba, a very loveable man, was a little different from the others; he was in poor health, illiterate, and knew very little English.

All the six accused were alleged to be members of the executive committee of K.A.U.; the first five certainly were, but I never believed that Karumba was, and felt that the government had probably charged him by mistake. The fact that the government had apparently singled out the executive committee of K.A.U. for prosecution supported the widely-held suspicion that part of their motive for the prosecution was to find a pretext for proscribing K.A.U. and thus depriving the Africans of all lawful political representation. They would not have dared to proscribe it without some such pretext; and they did in fact do so after the accused had been convicted.

The actual charges put forward were that Kenyatta had managed the proscribed organisation Mau Mau, and the others had assisted in the management, and that all of them were members of it. The maximum sentence was seven years' imprisonment, with the possible addition of a recommendation for "restriction", which entitled the Governor, after the expiry of the sentence, to restrict the accused indefinitely to residence within a designated area, as small as the Governor chose to make it.

As I have already related in Chapter 8, the government performed some tricks to get the trial held in a remote area, and its next problem was to find a magistrate to try it. There was not, and never had been, in the area it had selected, a professional magistrate. It had some trouble finding anyone to accept appointment as a resident magistrate to try the case, but in the end it appointed a former judge of the Supreme Court of Kenya, who had retired on reaching the age-limit, and was living in the Colony. He had the reputation of being a strong supporter of the colonial government, and of having the then usual racist attitude to "natives"; certainly, that is how he appeared to me in the three months I appeared before him in the case.

He took up the hearing on the 24th November, 1952, and adjourned it until the 3rd December, by which date I was expected to be, and was, present. On that date, by way of an early and a bad illustration of the way in which he was going to favour the prosecution, he refused to order the prosecution to give any particulars of the charges, which were stated in the charge in the vaguest possible way, mentioning no acts of any kind, and giving the widest dates possible, beginning with the date when Mau Mau was proscribed and ending with the date when the accused were detained under the "Emergency" over two years later. Thus, the accused were told nothing whatever beyond the words of the section of the Penal Code and the name of the proscribed society which they were alleged to have managed. Had the magistrate made the order for particulars, one can judge by the evidence which was later given that the prosecution would have been in grave difficulties, for it had then only a vague idea of what it hoped to prove.

If one looks at all the evidence that was in the end given, and assumes for the moment that it was true, what did it prove? To start with negatives, there was never any evidence, good or bad, which connected any of the accused with Mau Mau in any tangible fashion. It was never said where Mau Mau's head-quarters were, how it was organised, who were its officers or leaders, what was its constitution, or any such matter, nor was it shown that any of the accused had ever attended a meeting of its executive or indeed of the organisation at all. No witness ever said that he was a member of Mau Mau, an informer, who could prove what Mau Mau did. The evidence which was called covered some twenty-two miscellaneous and unconnected incidents, which the prosecution invited the judge to hold to amount, when all the bits and pieces were looked at together, to proof of the charges.

Of these twenty-two incidents, which fell into several groups, three were presumably regarded by the prosecution as the most important, two of them being the first on which evidence was called: they were alleged ceremonies of installation into Mau Mau, said to have been carried out by Kenyatta himself; they were both said to have taken place several months *before* Mau Mau was proscribed. (There were two other alleged initiation ceremonies in the whole case, but neither involved Kenyatta.) It is curious that no attempt was ever made to prove any initiation after Mau Mau was proscribed, especially when one bears in mind that, as was learnt in the end, the prosecution had no scruple whatever about calling perjured witnesses to tell invented stories.

The next group contained six incidents in which Kenyatta was alleged to have failed to denounce Mau Mau when he had an opportunity so to do, or to have told people "not to bother" about it. There was another incident, a little different, which the prosecution did not raise but the defence did, of an important speech by Kenyatta at a great public meeting, in which he did in fact denounce Mau Mau. Then there were a group of incidents, four in all, concerning some hymn books and a black note-book. The latter had been found in Kenyatta's house at the time of his arrest, but it was never shown that he had any connection with it; and the hymn books contained hymns praising Kenyatta, which were partly the same as some of those in the note-book. The remaining three incidents covered a story that in conversation Kenyatta had advised some of his followers not to administer oaths by force, another story that Kenyatta had mentioned Mau Mau as something with which he was somehow connected, at a time when the only witness concerned admitted that Mau Mau had never been heard of, and the last was a letter written four years before, inviting people to attend a meeting not of Mau Mau, which was in any case not then proscribed, but of the "Kikuyu Central Association".

Whether evidence of initiations or any other alleged Mau Mau activities before that body was proscribed could even be admitted in evidence was more than doubtful; to prove that a man managed a body when it was lawful, without proving that he did so after it was proscribed, is rather like proving that a man habitually drove fast along a road that had no speed-limit until one was imposed, and then never did so again. But the magistrate admitted the evidence, and relied on it.

The incident that in the end became most significant from the point of view of the credit or discredit of the whole prosecution was the first one, relating to an alleged initiation ceremony. The prosecution relied on the evidence of one witness, a man called Rawson Macharia, who told a story teeming with improbabilities and one or two impossibilities. He mentioned the names of nine other persons who, he alleged, had been present at the ceremony in addition to himself and Kenyatta. If the prosecution had asked these people for their version of the matter, they would have all have said that there was no truth in the story; but it did not ask them. The defence called all the nine people named by Macharia, and they all denied his story; and Kenyatta did so too. The magistrate found the incident proved, saying:

> "I disbelieve ten witnesses for the defence, and believe one witness for the prosecution. I have no hesitation whatever in doing so."

As appeared later, the story told by Macharia was a complete fabrication from beginning to end, and he was paid for it by the government pretty heavily with a free passage to the United Kingdom, a two years' course in local government at a British university, and two years' subsistence, and, as a bonus, a seat to view the coronation of the Queen, plus a promise of a post under the government on his return. The cash value of his reward for perjury, not including the post under the government, was £2,578. All these facts were proved from the mouths of government witnesses in a subsequent trial. But what could not of course be proved was how high up in the hierarchy of government the conspiracy to adduce perjured evidence went.

Other prosecution witnesses were shown at the trial to be manifestly unreliable with about the same cogency as Macharia, but none of them was subsequently unmasked in the way he was.

The magistrate convicted all the accused, sentenced them to the maximum of seven years' imprisonment, and recommended them for restriction. A number of appeal proceedings were carried through, with no more success than the acquittal of Achieng Oneko, who was immediately deprived of his freedom

K

by being "detained" under the Emergency Regulations; and all the others, after their terms of imprisonment were completed, were "restricted" until shortly before independence. The appeals went twice to the Privy Council on applications for leave to appeal, and on each occasion the then Lord Chief Justice, a man of strong character and devoted to the "establishment", whom I have already mentioned in Chapter 10 of Book 1, came especially to the Privy Council to take part in the hearing. His normal work was to hear cases in the High Court, but he was qualified to sit in the Privy Council, and left the High Court to do so. He played a prominent part in the arguments, and was generally thought to have been largely instrumental in getting the petitions dismissed.

I must now go back a little in time, to deal with some proceedings in Gibraltar. The story is a long one, but I feel that I must relate it here, as it illustrates so well both the British ruling-class behaviour in helping the fascists who were preparing for the Second World War and the similar smaller-scale behaviour of the judge and other officials of the little colony of "the Rock".

The cases had in a sense nothing to do with Gibraltar, for they were only dealt with there because in the summer of 1938 the British Navy seized a British merchant ship in a Spanish port and took it to Gibraltar as the nearest place where British jurisdiction could be brought to bear on it.

At that time the (ultimately successful) rebellion of Spanish fascists against the liberal Republican Government of the country, which started in 1936 and was powerfully supported with aircraft and ground troops by the two great fascist states of Europe, Italy and Germany, led to a great many legal and political problems, particularly in connection with the efforts of the legitimate government to buy arms. Its clear rights in international law both to buy arms wherever it could find a supplier, and to object to the supply of arms to the rebels, had been disregarded by Britain, Germany, Italy, and other powers, who had entered into a "non-intervention" agreement, under which they took steps to prevent arms being carried to the lawful government, whilst the Germans and Italians continued not only to supply the rebels but also took an active part in the war on the rebel side with their own forces, the British government turning a blind eye to their activities. Under the non-intervention agreement, "observers" were put on all ships trading to Spain, to see that arms were not carried; and some of these observers were Germans. The British government had put teeth into its wicked policy by an Act, passed in 1936, which provided that "no article to which this Act applies . . . consigned to or destined for any port or place in Spain shall be taken on board or carried in any ship to which this Act applies" (broadly, any British ships). The "articles to which this Act applies" were a narrow range of articles, all of which were munitions of one kind or another; many things which would ordinarily be regarded as munitions were not covered; this was probably due only to bad or hasty drafting.

The facts out of which the cases arose were that the s.s. *Stancroft*, a British ship sailing under time-charter, loaded a general cargo in Barcelona at the end of April and beginning of May, 1938, to be carried coastwise to Valencia. (At that time, the Franco rebels had reached the coast between Barcelona and Valencia, so that everything that would normally have gone from the one city to the other by land now had to go by sea.) The ship arrived safely at Valencia; but while she was lying there, in Spanish territorial waters, she was boarded (probably unlawfully) by a British naval officer, who compelled her to sail to Gibraltar. The British government must have been very malevolent, very cowardly, or very pro-fascist, or perhaps all three, to have instructed the Navy to treat vessels carrying goods coast-wise from one Spanish port to another as if they were carrying goods *to* Spain under the Act; and, as we shall see, she was in any case probably carrying nothing that fell within the Act at all.

When the ship reached Gibraltar, the authorities (probably unlawfully) discharged the whole of her cargo, giving neither the owners, the time-charterers, nor even the Master any opportunity to check or even to follow what they were doing. After discharge, the authorities retained 0·3 per cent of the cargo, which they suspected of falling within the terms of the Act, and re-loaded the rest. The Head of the Customs then questioned the Master, the other officers, and the "non-intervention" observer, a German; although criminal proceedings against the Master were plainly contemplated, he was given no warning of any kind—no caution, for example, that he was not bound to incriminate himself. The questioning was based on a wrong list of prohibited articles, which was much wider than that in the Act, and had no validity in English law. When the Master's lawyer demanded to be present, he was refused permission. The notes taken at this examination were never shown to the defence in the proceedings which were ultimately taken, and the Head of the Customs was not called as a witness; the excuses or explanations offered by the prosecution for not calling him were (a) that they thought that the defence might object to his evidence (which they could have found out by putting him in the witness-box, in which we had good reason to believe that he would have helped the defence considerably), and (b) that they thought he might have been damaged in cross-examination.

After some delay, in which one can guess that the not very competent authorities in Gibraltar were consulting the not very scrupulous authorities in London, the Master was arrested, bail was refused, and he was made to sleep on a plank bed in the prison, in spite of a medical certificate that in his then state of health imprisonment would be dangerous to him. He was released on bail on the following morning by the magistrates, in spite of the opposition of the prosecution. The charge was that, contrary to the Act, he "took and carried on board" his ship articles prohibited by the Act to "be carried in ships consigned or destined for a port or place in Spanish territory . . ., he being privy to the said contravention". Carriage of goods in infringement of the Act could lead both to fine and imprisonment for the Master if he were privy to the contravention, and to forfeiture of the goods involved. After some further delay, the prosecution informed the defence in respect of what goods the proceedings were being brought; four different classes of goods were involved, the most important of which were eight radial aircraft engines.

I, together with Geoffrey Bing, then a junior barrister and later Q.C., were engaged to defend the Master. Bing went out a few days before I did, in order to convince the regular magistrate that he ought not to hear the case himself, as he was bound to be affected by bias. Bing did this quietly and successfully, and I arrived a few days later to present the defence before two lay magistrates. The prosecution was faced with so many difficulties that the case should never have been brought, and I think that no prosecuting authority in England would have even attempted it.

The prosecution had to make good five points, and was probably unable to make good even one of them. The first was that in point of law the Act, which was aimed at prohibiting the carriage of goods *to* Spain, applied to the carriage of goods coastwise from Spain to Spain. On the well-established rule of interpretation that Acts imposing criminal sanctions should be interpreted strictly in favour of the accused, this point fell to be decided against the prosecution. The next point was that the goods involved, or some of them, fell within the narrow definition given in the Act; on this, opinions might differ, for some of the goods were near the dividing line, but the only goods where any real doubt was present happened to be goods to the shipment of which the Master could not be held to be privy. The next point was that the goods were "consigned to or destined for a port or place in Spanish territory"; here too the prosecution was very weak, for the goods were not "consigned" at all, as they appeared neither on the manifest nor on any bill of lading, having almost certainly been put on the ship by mistake; and goods can hardly be said to be destined for a place (which must mean "intended by the shipper to go to that place") if they were never intended to sail on the ship at all. The fifth and last point that the prosecution had to prove was that the Master was privy to the contravention (i.e., that he knew of and consented to the shipment of the goods in question). One might think that the prosecution could prove that much, for there the goods were, on the ship of which he was the Master; but in fact there were many difficulties here too. The master of a ship has little knowledge of what is loaded on his ship, especially when she is time-chartered and is carrying general cargo, which normally—as in this case—comes in cases; he does not usually supervise stowage. The prosecution did call as witnesses the German observer and the second officer of the ship; the senior magistrate in his judgement said of them, rightly enough: "These are the most unreliable witnesses I have ever heard. The observer was biased, prejudiced, and systematically hostile to everything which took place on the ship. The evidence of the second officer was of a most conflicting and lying character. In my view, no jury of reasonably-minded people would run the risk of accepting such evidence."

The magistrates dismissed the case on the first point, holding that the Act did not apply to coastwise carriage; thus our evidence did not have to be given. Had we had to call it, we should have made out a very strong case for the proposition that the radial engines and some cylinders that were the only other item of any importance had been shipped by mistake on this ship instead of on another that was being loaded at the same time near by.

We naturally thought that this was the end of the case, for the prosecution, if it had been able to persuade any Court of appeal that the first point should be decided in its favour, would still have all the other points to face, in the light particularly of the magistrates' view of the unreliability of two vital witnesses; but, as we shall see, the case was far from over. For the moment we had two important matters to see to; firstly, to get the ship away from Gibraltar safely, and secondly, to recover possession of the goods—for the government, without any justification, was refusing to give them up.

The practical difficulties for the ship were substantial. She was a slow unarmed merchant ship. At Barcelona or Valencia, she was fairly safe, except for air raids; but in Gibraltar, whither she had been taken against her will, she knew that there were two rebel gunboats waiting outside to sink her if she sailed, and the British government had fallen to perhaps the lowest level in all its history in the way of failing to protect British shipping off the coasts of Spain. So, when I got back to London, I telephoned to the Admiralty to ask how the ship would be protected, and was told by some civil servant that she would receive "the ordinary protection that all British ships get from His Majesty's Navy". In the light of the way ships were being shelled and sunk by the rebels at that time, I lost my temper—for once, at the right moment—and let fly: "You ——, if that is all you have to say, I'll plaster you and your —— Admiralty all over the front pages of the press tomorrow morning as a bunch of cowardly murderers." The result was that the First Lord of the Admiralty, the late Duff Cooper, subsequently Lord Norwich, sought me out at once, and told me that he was ordering two destroyers to convoy the ship from

Gibraltar to Valencia. (The beauty of this was that the total strength of the British Navy at Gibraltar at that moment was two destroyers.)

Next came the question of the goods; we were concerned only about the radial engines, excellent modern machines, the property of the legitimate government of Spain, which sent a formal demand to the Gibraltar government, demanding the delivery up of its property. This latter government now displayed the most insolent disregard of the sovereign state of Spain. It formally acknowledged some of the letters from the Spanish government, and did not even do that much for others. It never asked the Spanish government for information, nor gave any reason, excuse, or apology, for detaining the goods; and finally it took proceedings for the forfeiture of the goods, although it knew full well that the Spanish government, as a sovereign state, could not lawfully or properly be involved in litigation in a foreign Court. The proceedings took the form of an action, in which they gave the name of "the Attorney-General of Gibraltar" as plaintiff, and "the owners and parties interested in certain prohibited articles forming part of the cargo of" the ship. It asked the Court to order the forfeiture of the goods "for contravening the . . . Act", and added—by perhaps the most blatant lie ever appearing on a government writ—that "the owners or parties interested in the goods are unknown to the plaintiff". This was no doubt an attempt, utterly futile of course, to cover up the fact that the government knew perfectly well that the proceedings should not have been brought, since they were bound to be stayed on the objection of the Spanish government. By international law, normally observed by the Courts of every state, proceedings which involve a foreign sovereign state or its property must be stayed or dismissed unless the foreign state clearly consents to their being brought; and the Gibraltar government should never have started these proceedings without communicating with the Spanish government first and asking for its consent.

Accordingly, the Spanish government gave Notice of Motion in this new case for an Order setting aside the proceedings and directing that the goods be delivered up to the Consul-General of the Spanish government. This brought the Chief Justice of Gibraltar on the scene for the first time. He was a close friend of the rebel "government", which controlled all the Spanish territory around Gibraltar, which he frequently visited for the purpose of riding or hunting; and his behaviour throughout the proceedings left much to be desired. He was unable to get out of his plain duty to stay the proceedings, but he refused to order the delivery up of the goods, giving as his "reasons" a series of unjustified attacks on the Spanish government. When asked to award costs to the Spanish government, which had had to come to the Court to prevent its goods being forfeited, he refused and delivered a further and even worse tirade against the government, which led me not merely to protest strongly in open Court against his remarks, but to insist on remaining seated when he rose to leave the Court. He explained to me that it was customary for counsel to rise when the judge left the Court, to show their respect; and I replied from my seat that that was why I could not possibly rise.

That was the end of the Chief Justice's activity in the case, but it was not the end of the whole matter. The goods were ultimately released as a result of long negotiations, but with regard to the prosecution of the Master there was more to come. The Gibraltar government, having lost a case which it never ought to have brought, now added to its misbehaviours by entering an appeal from the decision of the magistrates. And here, too, the government behaved disgracefully. By the time the appeal was lodged, the two months' annual vacation of the Court was beginning, and the Chief Justice always spent the vacation outside Gibraltar, appointing the Attorney-General as his deputy meanwhile. This was done in this instance, and it did not seem likely to anyone that the appeal would be brought on until the following October. However the government, anxious to play every trick it could, suddenly brought the appeal on, probably in the hope that I would be on my vacation and would not be able to appear; but I managed to get there in time. One of the difficulties for the government was that the deputy Chief Justice, i.e., the Attorney-General, could not possibly hear the appeal as he had acted as counsel in the case; and it had accordingly to find another deputy. It of course wanted a deputy who could be relied upon to decide any and every point in its favour, and it took some time to find one; in the end it appointed one of its own minor officials.

Even the hearing was full of tricks; the points for argument were the validity of the appointment of the deputy, some other points of law, and of course the four points that had been before the magistrates. As no evidence was required on the appeal, it could all have been disposed of in two, or at the most three working-days; but the deputy (if he was validly appointed), played another trick. He announced that he would hear each point separately, and decide it before going on to the next point; there was nothing wrong in that, but on the first day, after the first point had been argued, and judgment had been given on it, the whole operation taking an hour and a half, the deputy announced that he would not hear the next point until the following day. I protested, but not very vigorously, as I assumed that this was only "for once". But I soon learnt that he proposed to deal with the whole case at the rate of one point per day, keeping everybody hanging about in the colony with nothing much to do for nine or ten days, in the course of which he would do about fourteen hours' work. I then protested with great vigour, but he refused to budge and gave no explanation for his conduct.

Point by point, and day by day, he decided everything against me, and allowed the appeal. This was not without its advantages for us, for the government could not arrest the Master, who had left the Colony with his ship long ago, and we could launch an appeal to the Privy Council, where we could not merely argue all our excellent points before competent judges but could expose fully all the rascalities of the Gibraltar government.

But here we had an undeserved misfortune; a fortnight before the appeal argument was to be heard, the Master died. As he was the sole appellant, and all criminal appeals against a man drop if he dies, the appeal could not be argued.

Index

Part 1: Law and Politics

Part 2: Law in the Colonies